from the warring factions

from the warring factions

Ammiel Alcalay

introduction by Diane di Prima

a conversation with Benjamin Hollander

edited by Fred Dewey

re: public / UpSet Press

Los Angeles —— New York

The new design, author's note, and preface by Diane di Prima were
created for the 2012 edition. The original 2002 edition was edited,
designed, and published by Fred Dewey for Beyond Baroque.

Excerpts of this book appeared in Crayon; Nocturnes; Jubilat;
Raddle Moon; Poeisis; Public Discourse; 110 Stories, an anthology
edited by Ulrich Baer (New York University Press, 2002); Nineteen
Lines: A Drawing Center Writing Anthology, edited by Lytle Shaw
(New York: Roof Books & The Drawing Center, 2007); and We
Begin Here: Poems for Palestine and Lebanon, edited by Kathy
Engel and Kamal Boullata (Northampton: Interlink, 2007)

re: public is an ongoing project dedicated to fostering and preserv-
ing principles of a democratic-republic in culture, thought, and the
public realm. This book is published and distributed in collabora-
tion with UpSet Press, an independent press based in Brooklyn. The
original impetus of UpSet Press was to upset the status quo through
literature. The press has expanded its mission to promote new work
by new authors; the first works, or complete works, of established
authors, including restoring to print new editions of important
texts; and first time translations into English. Established in 2000,
UpSet Press organized readings and writing workshops until 2005,
when it published its first book, Theater of War, by Nicholas
Powers. The University of Arkansas Press became UpSet's official
distributor in 2011. For more information, visit upsetpress.org.

With special thanks to André Spears.
Graphics consultant, Biotop 3000.

ISBN: 9780976014263
Library of Congress Control Number: 2012937087

Printed in the United States of America

for Srebrenica

CONTENTS

introduction by
Diane di Prima / i

from the warring factions

1. Old Bridge / 1
2. no place / not rome / 17
3. migration / hegira / 55
4. borrowed time / 91
5. night of unity / 131

*

a conversation with
Benjamin Hollander / 171

a note on materials
& processes / 215

further notes,
addenda, & bios / 223

introduction by Diane di Prima

I agreed to write an introduction to this book because I knew that it had touched my life in some profound and intimate way. That I return to it over and over. Of course, when I sit to write, it isn't easy. All I wanted to say was "This book forced me to redefine my life." But how?

I stood in the middle of my study, surrounded with my usual clutter: manuscripts, correspondence, junk mail and debris, notebooks, mostly un-typed and un-transcribed, tapes ditto, books half-read, for which there was no shelf space— what seemed the disarray of centuries—and I felt the familiar annoyance, the "can't you ever do anything right" *surge through me again, but this time that feeling hesitated, it paused slightly, lurched sideways an imperceptible inch.*

I had just been reading *from the warring factions*, and came with those eyes to my room, to some particular writing project, but the imperative I carried from my *warring factions* was that I had to somehow reconstruct my life, to see it differently. To tell myself a different story. For perhaps the first time I saw that from birth I had been at war, and that instead of blaming myself for "my mistakes", berating myself for the many losses: friends, work—mine and others'—(paintings, manuscripts, etc.) that had disappeared, been sold or destroyed or lost along the way—I needed to lighten up. *I saw it was a miracle that anything at all had survived, myself included. Any of the past. The work. The children. That anything had made it through at all.*

This is the gift of *from the warring factions*. It's no one page, no single breakthrough or juxtaposition, but Ammiel Alcalay's way of bringing the intimate and the political into the single arena where neither could be identified as itself— where "it was not art but some memorial like ice" is balanced by a profound understanding: that I, that perhaps all of us, have lived our lives in a war zone—that each struggle is no more or less than any other. That if definition of a life:

a woman's, an artist's, a warrior's life, is possible—it is not in counting defeat or loss but in realizing what one has managed to hold onto. To pass on. There is no aspect of ourselves, of flesh & relatedness—however hidden—that is not marked, scarred & seared by this battle, the singular battle of this time. And *yet we feel.* We are not estranged from what we love & beauty as reason, as Source and goal —has not been obliterated from the battlefield.

The Beloved's face can yet be traced, albeit in ash & broken glass, *trobar clus* weaves barely audible through screams of the wound, shouts of the dying and the possible. *Hyacinthos* pushes to bloom through the mouth of an unnamed corpse, and all true Victory is secret.

from the warring factions

1.

OLD BRIDGE

Miró is in The Museum of Modern Art.

Míro is in Sarajevo.

A famous playwright is on stage at Symphony Space and over the air on NPR.

The announcer calls me twice during a break to find out how to pronounce the name Izeta.

Izeta is Míro's wife.

They have a dog.

It is December 1st, 1993.

Certain people say we should always go back to nature.
I notice they never say we should go forward to nature.
It seems to me they are more concerned that we should
go back, than about nature. If the models we use are the
apparitions seen in a dream or the recollection of our
prehistoric past, is this less a part of nature or realism
than a cow in a field? I think not.

The role of the artist has always been that of image maker.
Different times require different images.

Today, when our aspirations have been reduced to a desper-
ate attempt to escape from evil, and times are out of joint,
our obsessive, subterranean and pictographic images are
the expression of the neurosis which is reality. To my mind
certain so-called abstraction is not abstraction at all,
on the contrary, it is the realism of our time.

Adolph Gottlieb

1947

no pyramids dot the skyline

in the seats of power of

this crumbling empire

the ghosts of industry eat
this old half city bridge
of nevermore again
eat Glamoć and
Grahovo
eat these
years

posters of Sadaam whirl and spin
stealth bombers drop TVs
over Baghdad books
burn in Sarajevo
babies choke
in clouds

of evaporated milk
the ghosts of industry

dot this landscape

lo these many years of construction repairing
the irreparable potholes the gaping erosion of
industrial repetition this tarred and feathered
landscape this tarred and feathered history

my neighbor found an arrowhead in
his backyard 385 10th st. Brooklyn

waking up in a sweat I found the Old Bridge hanging
from my neck and the whole town of Počitelj
in the pocket of my jacket draped over a
chair in the shadow of a pot filled with
rosemary and lavender

gazing at sailors dying for trust together as light plays
through the leaves when you least expect a burning desire
in ways we could hardly even articulate attached to no real
itinerary eyes too slow to shelter too close to part

our park just souvenir feathers drawn across states skin taut
across manifest destiny listening ear to the ground for what
isn't there evidence of beauty evidence destroyed everywhere
desire and hunger taxis with amulets evoke wounds across
time within earth underground too slow to penetrate too
late to spawn such a chaste upbringing such sheltered
accents for no language escapes

warm stone cold stone rooms at either end and the room in
the middle of this journey dank and mouldy elegant and even
gentrified now but a poor room a room for the poor a room
to end up in bones creaking and lungs clogged the hard life
embedded in the very body of the city in gold adorned and
manner straightforward her head covered like the dome a
part of her very body you would have to rip the eyes out
of to destroy the memory of "fourteen of us" in this room

neither owl nor eagle nor deer

only feathers on a souvenir drum bought from an
Algonquin speak parking lots and minarets toppled
to dust ponds and rivers Mashpee next to Barnstable
and Sandwich speak for the garbage we help

attracted by trolleys a view of the
river imagine escutcheons herald
aluminum arms door knob or handle
either grip the very same even this
oblong sea that ocean grandfathers
on the move underground the bloody
corpse gnawed and nibbled at by
tourists of fortune caution stop
words kill writer ahead by the dead
hand of heraldry of glories past and
yet to come feel the weight of this
token in my hand in yours holding
mine the night the bombing began the
night we decided to kill the garden to
bury Eve forever to starve her children
starve her veiled sisters Night and
Layla who'll never find the prince
that opened a cookshop in Damascus
her groom and lover who left his
turban by the bedside to go to the privy
only to find a hunchback up to his ears
in shit caught headfirst by a demon
lost in a makeshift trial of trials and
tests and travail and wandering in the
whirlpools of space commandeered
by our own obsequious hosts gearing
up at every idle moment to steal not
only life but even air itself don't you
see / we're on the eve of destruction

unlikely
intimate
unraveling
toy wrapping
the daily tide

our park
manifest

disappearing city
injured at the outset astute
observers anonymous random
kitchen speak for the garbage we help

on the river of joy and
when time comes
and on the day of jewels
and upon a crown of wealth
and depths of poverty not
my own none of
this surprise me

she sang

2.

no place

not rome

(for Jerry Estrin 1947-1993)

"Haglund knelt down and traced the dimensions of
the grave in the dust caked to the side of his vehicle.
In another time and place, he could have been Virgil
mapping out his descent through the circles of hell."

race the cold scent this urge this rough fell the map

meander through dust in this vein like an ace

in the hole an ache in the hole the ides rave

sown in the soft web like gout nickle and dime

oh me oh my the other sons the tot oh soft us

owned and raced and rough and oh so cold

in this our day of darkness see what beyond the scattered
leaves the Sybil said no time to gape at games the place
that once was across the waters the shores that lie beyond
the blurry lines going away like things spent to live in the
very glint of what little might have been paradise such
blood and dreams there don't seem to be any civilians
face about face I don't care about the imperial mouthpiece
doesn't need any face to fight his war I don't read about
that stuff in the line of duty in the line of destiny without
losing control to speculate about what may or may not be
included in a plan that might or might not be implemented
is inappropriate in this secret room drawing now if to
sympathize or if to despise this empire of dreams dreaming
of empire and blazing fields in the fearful hearts of such
good people heaping much more on their plates than they
can eat these are the innocents over and over again they
claim they have no one to talk to—"rested and resolute,"
"calm and resigned," "determined and vigilant," "steady and
strong" a life which does not need war would go up used
like destiny to always learn the passion for the justice things
not sufficiently heroic buildings taken out on the way to work
collapsing in this bitter inheritance of caliber and alchemy
this heaving breast of sleep and horn and ivory

lulled to sleep along our watch

(as when a broadcast, tightly controlled by
conquering censors, begins transmission, word
for word the listener battles each instinct to reach
for reason and intellect, to fend off the impending
enclosures that occupy seeing or hearing all images
of division cut along the lines of any other fabric)

"they should be soaking in oil"

"olives?"

"birds?"

"A line drawn in the sand, a line

To arrive"

"this is no country battle"

"my brother

my seemingness"

"of what dead comrade did the priestess speak?"

"what body did she mean for them to bury?"

"So much for human precautions. Next came attempts to appease heaven. After consultation of the Sybylline books, prayers were addressed to Vulcan, Ceres, and Prosperpina, Juno, too, was propitiated. But neither human resources, nor imperial munificence, nor appeasement of the gods, eliminated sinister suspicions that the fire had been instigated. To suppress this rumor, Nero fabricated scapegoats—and punished with every refinement the notoriously depraved Christians (as they were popularly called). Their originator, Christ, had been executed in Tiberius' reign by the governor of Judaea, Pontius Pilate. But in spite of this temporary setback the deadly superstition had broken out afresh, not only in Judaea (where the mischief had started) but even in Rome. All degraded and shameful practices collect and flourish in the capital."

the capital the capital this is the Appian way speed up
the process by showing your "empress" this page don't
be too stubborn to ever show a sign make like Nero in
QUO VADIS shorts eight fiery patterns blazing in color
poor toga clad Nero never knew the smart comfort of
these full-cut rayon boxers he don't know what he
missed the small voice of Cleopatra whispering to Liz
across the centuries: "You really can rule the world.
Get a barge! Roll yourself up into a magic carpet and
have it sent to" SO many fascinating possibilities parallels
in life of the two girls spooky both queens accused of stealing
husband from nice wife: Liz replies—What am I supposed
to do, ask him to go back? Cleo would have done the same
in Cinemascope the modern miracle you can see without
glasses without sympathy without tyranny without oil the
orgies the triumphs the palaces the costumes the pomp
sails on ship of state as you blaze your way through the gulf
the brush-grass and the sand the trench and the cities of
salt liken my weeping eye to a casting of the stones to a
bewildering darkness on fire with hunger the tent marks
worn away and left to the wild uncovered like the script
of faded spools disintegrating reels wound in spirals of dust
as forms begin to reappear at the limits of weariness travel-
ing on a pillow of thick oil or black pitch before the wheel of
war turns down the departing riders like the flat back of a
shield no one dares cross when the chameleon struck by heat
begins to reel and twist its head the camels like boats
floating down the desert of the Tigris

"Productive labor was carried on more and
more by slaves while the free rural and urban
workers fell into unemployment, drifted to Rome,
where they lived as vagabonds upon the public
supplies of corn, were kept in a good humor by the
public games, and used as voting cattle:

'The wild beasts of Italy have their caves to retire to, but the brave men who spill their blood in her cause have nothing left but air and light. Without houses, without any settled habitation, they wander from place to place with their wives and children, and their generals do but mock them when, at the head of their armies, they exhort them to fight for their sepulchres and household gods, for among such numbers there is not perhaps one Roman who has an altar that belonged to his ancestors or a sepulchre in which their ashes rest. The private soldiers fight and die to advance the wealth and luxury of the great, and they are called masters of the world, while they have not a foot of ground in their possession."'

so many romes to go

o rome of scots
and rome of brits
of slavs and spics
jewrome arabrome
romeafrique
no can go home
no mo rome

o rome

the gold standards draped in purple gleam already it seems
I see the regal brothers standing before the people of Rome
the earth has opened a path for you where ever there are
living things you are also there what was only a world you
have made a city year by year the green earth comes up
from below meadows and groves folded closely together
the gift not now water from a well but the tablet itself the
verse graven on imperishable gold caught in the tangle
these are the names that extend the memory of sorrow
a bush a bird a fish with scales that gleam in the ocean
the crown I longed for without looking back when the
sun was up the forgotten maze of things obsolete like
strains marshalled to a dance appear to me as you do
pull your radiant hair back as things descend upon us
and we remember the splendid movement of the old
power returning may your wounds close and heal
because you have ignored the journeying after eager
feet flown to the circle desire out of the weary wheel
out of the pure below in vain blood stains this river
with your bow and quiver hanging from your
shoulders like a kid fallen into milk I have paid
the penalty and receive here the armor of memory

"here, happily unoppressed with any civil bondage,
without any military establishments, without
governors or any masters but the laws"

"to see, contemplate and study
    the world, the spectacle of it"

"the love or the hate of it" "every
    hope of reparation and freedom"

"each and all" "the words and deeds"

      "to work hard" "to sustain and abstain"

                to wish "with all my faculties

                that the social wealth

                would belong"

"as it was the fruit of the work of all"

      "I know that, I see that, I tell that to everybody"

      Orpheus too was afraid—

      "it was a night without moon"

                      "I remember":

"come along, lead your poet through the grass, we will
follow you—forget about the courts and their turmoil,
the din of the cities, the noise of war and the greed
that makes men sailors"—AND CUT TO:

Villafalletto Cavour Torino

dishwasher tailor pastry cook candy maker stone
pits brickyards railroads construction gangs ditch

digger pick and shovel man ice cutter fish
peddler labor agitator license plate painter

New York Meriden Springfield
Worcester Plymouth Mexico
Dedham Charlestown
Bartolomeo
Vanzetti

"These fruits also remember to me the home's garden. At the time I lived there this kind of peaches was very little known. I remember when my father planted the first tree of this kind, in my garden. I tasted few of its fruit before to left my native place."

"oh, gíve me a hóme

where the búffalo róam

where the déer and the ántelópe pláy

where séldom is héard

a díscóuraging wórd

and the skíes are not clóudy all dáy"

"No. It's not true…One day…there will be no more frontier. Then men like you will go too. Like the Mohicans. [pause] And new people will come. Work.
Struggle to make their light," like:

(Tom no Roman
iceman Iacavone
last such man in
New York City
last at least a
century last at
least a cemetary
last at least as
long as sixty acres
of buildings
and bricks and
beams and signs
going bye-bye
nineteen-sixty
seven no imaginary
mitla no maginot
no bar lev line)

O ROMEO

where art thou
if I kiss this wall
does it not stain this soil
these bricks *my* palestine
these bricks *my* olive-trees these
bricks *my* figs these bricks
my wild thyme

as in winter many times have I set out early in
fear or in desire my face the day drenched in
immunity till the trees be bare bereft of leaves
I am known as you have come to know me
"not that I condemn my former way, but that
this is more proper to my present purpose" as
I bring them back to life with your memory the
occasion fair and the subject pleasant "to set
forth what must be done" "by the putting
together of figures" "symbols of human
voice" "the power to recall past events"

in the procession

    the regal procession

               "Plato's always cold"

       retreat underneath

       a heap of charms

       a game of

       chicken

         a father's arms

to walk among them the migrated I mean
to take leave take such leave exceptionally
gifted honor the given common property
the commonwealth this tour of shields
these battle lines drawn by shepherds
loads and loads of junk heaps of
stones of hornets zephyrs
mercurys and ramblers
of hudsons pontiacs
and oldsmobiles
lodes and lodes
of tin and
copper
dice

dangling
off a broken mirror:
leaving no leaving was never part of the plan
just suppose none of it ever happened that way
the stations closing the hopeless dirge the mortal
fury dying unrooted the bells the bells the infernal
clanging of the bells jarring more than order this frame
this shrill and hollow frame none there to raise the wonder
to strike the shell for truth for chairs for caves given angels
begetting and begotten numbering days and dwelling and
building the idols of the cave and the idols of the market
and the idols of the tribe and the idols of the theater sightseeing
asleep at the wheel on the solstice and the equinox a brother
in the field and another in the smithy one a nomad and the
other forging brass and iron back when you had to have
a killer in the family to handle a lyre or touch a flute you
claim not to have been there but "the tuneless tribe" "and
"fish of the sea" "built tireless eyes" "having fastened them
together with clamps of affection" disdainful indignant
"of night" "lonely" "gazing at the sacred circle" "as when
fig-juice binds white milk" and "limbs wandered alone"
"the divided meadows of Aphrodite" "first by the tall olive
trees" and "sweet seized on" bitter and "bitter rushed toward"
sweet so enamored of ourselves so enamored of the machine
so ignorant so arrogant so passive struck underneath this
fury of mortal arms "I wept and wailed when I saw the
unfamiliar land" "and the black color in the bottom of
a river that arises from the shadow" the charge to dwell again
in fury and retreat "and in so far as the rarest things came
together in their fall" "how great the honor, how deep
the happiness" "as if we could invent liberty" sharp
and hopeless compass to raise or mend this race

"The studio, its war films"

"The park"

"Or the frontier then, along with some angels falling":

"I will write something,

a meditation perhaps,

and name it":

"a little knowledge of the past":

Somehow she breathes easier because he's there. She's in a white shirt with the sleeves rolled up. He leads her away from some of the people and takes her hand. She is awakening to a new spirit, a new wind blowing through a new land, a new self-determination... She's drawn to this rough yet graceful man with his direct manner. He settles against a wall. She leans next to him. Their shoulders touch. To her everything about him seems to be somehow right. She's discovered that the passions and outrage that move him, move her... And her readiness to give herself to what stirs the deepest resonances of her soul is the same as his. He looks at her. She's beautiful in the firelight. Her eyes find his and she folds into his arms. His lips find hers and tears stream down her face. She's suffused with an elation she can't explain. In the night before doomsday a romance is born in rebellion amid the huddled people in this small stockade ripped from the black earth of the forests of a wild continent:

of no place

not Rome

3.

migration / hegira

I moved as free as light and as we sailed that strange
boat my dreams were fire like many voices walking forth
to awake the ruined labyrinth the motions of the crew
struggling until the stars spread from every tent I knew
that ship once made all things subject to its power as if
it drowned in remembrance and left the shades the only
living thing token flowers on the ground that night we
moved towards home a robe of glory beyond the sun
beyond the stars on the verge of formless space the grate
of brass the brazen rust the shadow in which friends return
like birds from the world's raging sea invested with the light
of language accents sounds a sense of actual things to weave
it was not art but some memorial like ice still clung to me
she was all I had her willing feet followed where I went
in the murmur of her dreams like the secret bird my hand
not a ghost's but warm with human blood these words had
fallen the secret of this world pierced as if the light was not
withdrawn for ever the past come again like wonder our
scattered tribes no longer blind cast off their memories
descending on still waters as whirlpools draw all wrecks
to their chasm to unfold to hear a strange and awful tale
the likeness of a shape a trace in gold imagined silver the
ages bear away those subtle nets which snare the living and
the dead of history as others know all its many names this
was ours the knowledge and the power justice a glance as
keen as lightning its shade a war that never failed to lick its
yellow light of wisdom to gaze on their spent and faded
luster woven beneath the veil like shelter in the desert

land of tide
between sea
beneath water
between land
where it stands out to sea
there it is grassy
at the spread out place
at the top of a rock
at the stone ledge
at the greater cove
beyond the mountain
at the red rock
at the falls into salt water
at the rocky slope
at the half way
that which is green
is far out
three upright
late in the night
it runs all out
at the island
it is day
there is no water
the summer is high
far advanced
I carry it out
go from my family
spend the fall of a year
in such a place
coming to the same time
I fulfill or accomplish it
put or make it equal
regain what I had lost

but the people
the procession regal
by origin and birth you are
of the land of leaving the unexpected owing
no one anything but the people in the fall "when the
hunter shoots the bear" and "its blood turns the leaves red"
the shields retreat migrate the battle lines common "the wood
wherein we walk" this division we have not always known this
plenty "journeying in your old age through every risk" "as the
slaves march on" to "see the site of the great old empire"
"unsuspected, dying, well-beloved, saying to the people,
do not weep for me, this is not my true country" this
muddy water the curved line a river valley circle within
a circle might mean very brave joined to a dwelling but
separated "moving secretly to the east" "not wasting any
time" "this time beyond the great tide-waters" "leaving
friends leaving family leaving hearts upon the ground"
"the map the voyage made" "to explain my detours" "to

keep them alive" "to resist the scheme" "like places desolate
of old" "in the lowest parts of the earth" "like the cities that
are not inhabited" "to the people of old time" "your bor-
ders are in the heart of the seas" on the morning star and
the evening star on the transit and the hood on the ornament
on the union on the rebellion and the shrillness that "will
never cease to trouble us" on "the western point of this
island" with its "variety of ochres of different colours,
with which the inhabitants paint their houses" against
autumn assembling "with weapons" "with symbols for
dwelling" with "four houses" with "our finest always dead"
with "the ravens that brought the prophet bread" dust
"where lies the passage strewn with yellow leaves" the
"horses that pass" the "leaves" "tangled" "in their manes"
having learned so to speak the words almond uncanny
evasive the stars not yours the "candles buried beneath
these waters" of "the door to the setting sun" between "all
you have seen on earth and all you can see now" the jaws
the knees the teeth buried in the mud "here you will find
your relatives" and your glory "laid waste" every precious
stone that was your covering the ruby the chrysolite and
the diamond the emerald the jade the sapphire the
turquoise the beryl and the gold the beads and braids and
coal-black hair "up and down in the midst of the stones of fire"
"coming from the east head first like arrows flying"
 "all the fish of the rivers" fallen "upon the open fields"
neither brought together nor gathered like ashes scattered
upon the earth blood in the streets and the wounded falling
in heaps "a king of kings from the north with horses and
with chariots and with horsemen" shall destroy your walls
and break down your towers and make you like a bare rock
as the sea causes waves to come up like a place for the
spreading of the nets in the middle of the sea and you
will search for the remains of your sons and daughters
left in the fields like dust in the midst of abundant waters

as a reed is shaken the ravens brought bread and meat in
the morning and bread and meat in the evening and the jar
of meal was not consumed neither did the cruse of oil fail
to save the horses and a great and strong wind rent the
mountains and broke the rocks in pieces horse for horse
and chariot for chariot in the high places where the women
wove covering to the sun and to the moon and to the planets
in the eleventh year she painted her eyes and adorned her
head and looked out at the window and he lifted up his face
and said who is on my side who and he said throw her down
so they threw her down and some of her blood was sprinkled
on the wall and on the horses and he trampled her under
foot and they went to bury her but they found no more of
her than the skull and the feet and the palms of her hands

I hardly dare to raise my voice itself as yet unknown in the
old way when you took your flight I thought of you on your
lonely journey the astounding nearness from the beginning
of the world to this day I scarcely know where to begin
among the inhabitants of the blaze we carried their seed
in the laden ship your name a shade left under where we
must feel it dark such subtle forms of affection and the
peculiar power to make us believe the executioner has
withdrawn his hand from the living which hear it as
an arrow shot out of a bow beyond the mark of day
into the confines of the night of those things which
are most known to us make to ourselves images of
memory dreams of war or of thunder torn in pieces
creased with a thousand circles like oil above water
the hideous roaring as if it had been an ordinary piece
of iron we build in a day dust we raise by our steps
no long sickness but worse than death the simplicity
you were born to all my endeavors like rivers pay
tribute as to the ocean years have come and gone
like the ship which bears me the ghost the dream
the shade of power a lasting chain a poison light
poisons the whole country now the line of war
extended by thirst of carnage driven and you
that bear the name of soldiers seek some new
trade for I cannot name all that I read of
sorrow on your worn faces our very
names which speechless memory
claims numbered among
the things that
are

"the sun and moon in their reckoning"

      "the star and trees bowed low"

            "the kernel in the grain and the fragrant herb"

the pear and plum trees so close to the window

    "like wool dyed and carded"

    "like scattered moths now left to the wild"

    "like inscriptions worn thin on flattened stones"

    "like tamarisks and boulders in the shimmering haze"

        love of the ruins inflames not my heart

        but the love of those who once inhabited them

"not so much the house but the roses:

they tear me apart"

in the *Search for Hidden Waters* you alone are guilty of my
death "like water over granite" "the conquest" "slipped over
the immensity" your turban was bound on your head but
no one could see you unredeemed caged in a city of refuge
you drew your sword from your scabbard and wielded it
against your enemies "my only librarie" "something it was
that now I have forgot" "a fire that shall consume all that
this stranger left" you bury him in the walls of your heart
under the shadow of your hand the hammer of my senses coated
with rust you would shield me from distress "the sweetness
and the ash" "but here" "in striking the tent to plant it in
a form more solid" "the stone crumbles and the water
penetrates" "ships sail through the market place" "a thread
of linen splinters a bar of iron" "water blazes like wood"
and "These letters, lines, and periured papers / all shall
burne to cinders in this pretious flame" "until time mend
again what it had twisted" "put out of mind" "all it has
ruined" "as streams return in the desert" "And from mine
ashes let a Conqueror rise / That may avenge this treason"
"set apart the lead from the gold" "knowing you are still
with me in my deep grief" "because no one cared to
check the time" and "they say there are two versions"
"the one talking of signs of hesitation" "and the other
talking of signs of defense"

"have you considered the water you drink?"

"the fire you kindle?"

"the birds above spreading their wings and closing them?"

"as if they were the stumps of fallen trees"

because the world was watching I personally never expect-
ed to "resist the scheme which commanded us to forget the
legendary" it was myself seemed held and lifting it would
be like pouring oil on an already burning fire at the sound of
the cry of the pilots no stone will be on another stone in the
southern part it was very strange a kind of dead silence for
they say "the breasts of the free are the graves of secrets" and
"questions of industry and idleness" demonstrate that if we
aim our action at "the presence of the real" and "the messages

of the unknown events, heroes" and "records of the earth,"
"then the sun of witnessing shines down" and "if I am like
them in the rest, I should resemble them in that" keeping
the peace but not enforcing it to save a town dating back to
Roman times for some reason at those moments you have no
brain you are so obedient that you just do what they tell you
"Take the sign down Do I have to tell you ten times Get up
there and take the sign down" the level of proof has not to be
different than any crime committed "is this for my wife" "yes
for you and your wife" "thank you very much" for days are
long they have judged and they have refused to consider
fruitless and sweet the rewards "they reject to be worthless"
muddy shoes a pair of jeans some moccasins a piece of wire
and a leather jacket aimed decisively "at the point where the
religious and social structure is most fragile" we refer here "to
the women, especially adolescents, and to the children" "Don't
be afraid" "I want to help you" "Your people need not die"
"Just decide what you want to do" "No matter if you're old or
young you'll get transport" for "whoever is effaced by the real
from confirmation is returned to the witnessing of others and
affirmed in the ravines of distinction" and "some people
mean by the moment the time in which a person happens to
be" certainly with hindsight we would never allow ourselves
to be the victims of double dealings for "absence is the
absence of the heart from the knowledge of the states that
are occurring" "due to the preoccupation of the perception
with what is coming upon it" "the minimum that it can
create is that of the principle of uncertainty these people
doing what they have done and knowing of our existence"
in the days leading up to the tragedy no one even complained
as they walked toward the gates they just walked through
in the final analysis overrun as part of an overall settlement
the enclave may not have been defensible

"his hand on my shoulder,

still trembling"

looked upon from the green earth the plain the city
the scattered camps the evening most clear and beautiful
calm as a cradled child sitting beneath pomegranates dates
and figs to know as others know the past world these sights
the few mysteries the signs concealing a nameless sense of
fear of speechless beauty these wonders which were weapons
none could share that spot suddenly stained the air like
burning emerald the likeness of a shape as swift as smoke
the darkness of brief frenzy the murmur the green light
the wild flowers like tokens fallen among the leaves

"to awaken public hope"

"in the tide of human things"

"which,

       like an epidemic transport" "can unlock

       with the slightest motion"

          "eat with poisonous rust into the soul"

    "the historical fact from which liberty

    derives all its recommendations,

    and falsehood the worst features

    of its deformity"

"the faithlessness of Tyrants" "the massacre and extermination of the Patriots" "the victory of established power; the consequences of legitimate despotism—civil war, famine, plague, superstition" "an utter extinction of the domestic affections"

"the judicial murder of the advocates of Liberty"

"the treachery and barbarity of hired soldiers"

tigers falcons hawks scorpions grey wolves black swans
yellow ants white eagles horses of fire autumn rain alley
soot dušan the great green legion red berets jokers knights
visors weekenders armada force flash troops commander
turtle slavonian shock mosque doves captain dragan six
districts mecet's babies drago's group glava's unit risto's
paras hasan's forces garibaldi's guys russian mercenaries
kozara brigade adolf rambo višegrad militia webbed masks
black gloves black ribbons large black cowboy hats and white
cloth tied around the left shoulder masked with camouflage
and distinct insignias black wool caps and green uniforms
with patches on both sleeves the right-arm patch a grey wolf
the left-arm patch bearing the four S's all black except for
the words Black Legion in white letters all blue and black
except red berets and arm patches white wolves black
headbands and fingerless gloves brown battle fatigues
lillies scarves olive fatigues beards and green berets black
clothing with a round unit patch on the sleeve a black
swan penetrating a woman lying on her back Special Unit
in white letters above the picture and underneath in black
letters the words Black Swans no insignia except a metal
plate on the shoulder bearing the name Captain Dragan
headbands or scarves and hats with fatigues bearing the red
white and blue flag of the Federal Republic or the National
Army star on the left front pocket stocking masks with eagle
patches or bands on the shoulders black uniforms military
or civilian clothes with headbands hats black berets or
flight caps bearing insignia: JNA HOS SDA SDP MOS
BSA HVO MTD SPS SRS SPO CDU SOS SKA

"Once a draft of the chronology was completed, a team of analysts was assembled to examine the information. One, for example, was assigned the task of collecting all information pertaining to specific targets shelled. Working with this information he prepared a map identifying specific locations of shelled targets reported. Other analysts prepared a list of the most frequently hit targets; a table of frequency of shelling, by division into designated areas, to determine those most frequently shelled. They also accumulated and identified photographs picturing targets shelled. Statistical analysts then examined the numerical data contained in the chronology.

"As part of their effort, statistical charts were prepared recording total daily shelling activity; daily numbers of persons killed; daily numbers of persons wounded; and combined reported shelling activity and casualties by day and by week. In preparing this statistical information, only reports in the chronology with daily totals (e.g. total number of persons killed on a given day, or total number of shells fired) were included. This methodology was utilized to prevent incomplete data from being factored into the daily averages computed.

"After an initial review of the statistics and the other data, it became apparent that a possible connection existed between the increase and decrease in shelling activity and related political events such as negotiations, meetings, preparations for negotiations, the hardening or softening of public positions by international and local leaders, and changes and potential changes of positions by certain governments. The relevance of this connection is that it establishes a possible link between military and political activities or objectives. With this fact in mind, a graph was created to track significant local and international events with the level of shelling."

"add war to war" not as an obstacle, but as an instrument
of its aims flawed from the beginning "principle, timeliness
and substance" stood in the way heightening the risk
images "rendered useless" blur the distinction raise unrealistic
expectations exceed the context of the present mandate
shrink the pocket:

say hello
to Ibrahim
left behind
the prism
of "moral
equivalency"

Alpha
Delta
Charlie
Mike
Papa
Sierra
Kilo
Hotel
Quebec
Foxtrot
November
Echo
Romeo

engage the column in accordance with agreed procedures
"holding all the cards" a consensus absent lacking a strategy
burdened by an unclear mandate forced to chart its own
course A light option without formed units A light option
with formed units A heavy option lift and strike building
on the process in order to promote symbolic deterrence
participate in the delivery enable force-multiplying
characteristics monitor significant blind spots "take stock"
and in the absence of fundamental consent "level
the killing field" and execute the mandate

In some cases, the victims were made to dig their own graves. In others, they were shot while standing in them. It appears that, over the course of the next several months, the bodies were taken out of the initial mass graves, and reburied in 33 different "secondary sites."

One survivor later realized that he was walking on blood

the slow agonies of legal torture a net of famine in the gulf of
hell armies divide the arrows of the plague eclipse the light
of other minds pierce free thought like lice day after day
the burning sun rolled on over the death-polluted land
soon the dust drinks that bitter dew the vulture and the
wild dog the snake the wolf and hyaena eat in horrid truce
the continent a zone of ruin bound by flame obediently
they came the multitude of hired assassins moving heartless
things the wasted fields beneath their feet the glutted beasts
and mangled gore streaming through the city each well
choked with naked corpses spotted with nameless scars
many saw their own lean image near the great fountain in
the public square where the living hid the dead a crumbling
pyramid and strange disease did glow in their green eyes
birds perished in the green woods scattered flocks and
herds died moaning fish poisoned in the streams
thrown petrified upon the shore

morning broke like iron shapes which fled in wonder
shadows which pursued a sound like thunder the roots of
the sea out of a burning oven columns and shapes like
statues and the state of kingless thrones that wild bird a
poisoned robe the eagle and the air as if some living thing in
the fountains of my life like sweet reality when the rain of
winter of questioning lingers a source appears like a green
home and sitting there alone I was no longer mad the blood
stood still delusion in my memory and all its shapes possessed
by thoughts which could not fade my prison was the earth
made desolate grief was meaningless I found a woman wan-
dering the streets as she heard my steps she leapt on me and
glued her burning lips to mine I took the food she offered so I
might be free of hope we passed without a word one shape of
many names the shade the pattern like a mine I rifled
through and through to track the steps of freedom its
secrets a subtler language from which I drew the power to
make immortal the disastrous frame of all I read of sorrow

to the North I saw the town on fire the fearful glow of bombs
flared overhead and the stain of steel like rain a killing rain
the heaps whose stony eyes glared in the morning light
defenceless limbs beneath our footsteps the wind our
screams alone the hill gave shelter a fiercer combat raged
beside me like a mad dog's hanging thirst the few who
survived fled trampling over the fields the shape swayed
like the sweet source of water the murmur ground the rocks
dust for ever haunted by those who stood within that ruin like
ghosts which come and go the wintry loneliness of those dead
leaves a thirst a knowledge came on us our very names which
speechless memory claims through the morass to which it
lent the sickness made still around my heart a voice shielded
us from our own cold looks a wide and wild oblivion as
the great Nile feeds Egypt the anguish of her mute and
fearful tenderness nursed us in the haunts where knowledge
her voice once again beside the fountain in the market place
the garments white a heap of worthless walls life fled within
those dwellings the vacant air the salt the bitterness the
strength of madness silent and stark amid that ghastly
waste the sun warm and all that now a strange tale of
strange endurance like broken memories
of many a heart woven into one

suddenly like shapes of living stone clothed in the light of
dreams I tore the veil the shrouds which wrap the world
the frost of death the flood of tyranny a paradise of flowers
within which the poor heart loves to keep the earnings
of its toil a common home stains of inevitable crime
pride built upon oblivion to rule the ages that survive
our remains violence and wrong an unreturning stream
the grief of many graves snow and rain on lifeless things
this is not faith or law opinion more frail or life poisoned
in its wells that delights in ruin as endless armies wind
in sad procession the earth springs like an eagle even
as the winds of autumn scatter gold in the dying flame
we learned to steep the bread of slavery in tears of woe
these faded eyes have survived a ruin wide and deep
which can no longer borrow from chance or change
what will come within the homeless future that gold
should lose its power and thrones their glory that love
which none may bind be free to fill the world like light
whose will has power when all beside is gone faint accents
far and lost to sense of outward things some word which
none here can gather yet the world has seen a type of peace
some sweet and moving scene returning to feed on us
as worms devour those years come and gone like the ship
which bears me in this the winter of the world

4.

borrowed time

'Twas mercy brought me from my pagan land,
Taught my benighted soul to understand.

Phillis Wheatley
1768

It is most unpleasant work to steal bones from
a grave, but what is the use, someone has to do it.

Franz Boas
June 6, 1888

this vast machine its transient sweetness expectant
the acts recovered when action ceases and ideas range
in due order we see the long forgotten years long departed
all their cunning all their strength all their force more
guarded the owl seeks the caves of night in sadness
the unbounded regions of the mind the land of errors
which wanton Tyranny with lawless hand had made
of wrongs and grievance unredressed till nature leave
the earth behind and place itself would rise and overspread
the lands beneath and learn to imitate her language there
bright jewel final wreck fatal sceptre I strive to comprehend

even the most commonplace objects seemed to have
some bearing on his destiny:

the word lure—rebel for blues or stripers

"the shift from fresh air to our political atmosphere"

"Like the miner's canary"

"not a grant of rights to
but a grant of rights *from*:

a reservation of those not granted."

"as the snow melts before the sunbeam"

"a sketch in red crayon"

"the good name of our country"

"mica"
"volcanic glass"
"chalcedony"
"conch shells"
"shark teeth"
"copper"

like "loosely gathered rope" "flung across open water"

"from boat to boat"

their memories, it can now be asserted, were authentic:

    "inhaling the smell of antiseptic and the stench of bedpans,
    listening to the mumblings of the dying, lying in bed
                   watching the beautiful boats"

    "To a man, they said, they were disappointed"

He couldn't remember if they had thrown pebbles or sand at each other. He saw her legs for a second, then again as they appeared under a chassis or though a door. He played with her on the swings across the street from the garage, the swing she flew off as she ran across the field telling him she'd beat him to the junkyard. He chased her over, through the white fence, across the street, past the gas pumps and the air hose, trudging through the mud by the tin shacks whose doors rattled and swung in the wind all the way to the yard filled with ancient, smashed cars. She ran through them, opening doors, jumping across hoods and roofs, taunting him with sand or pebbles. Glass crunched and doors rattled as he landed running, sand hitting hollow fenders as it crumbled and spread to the ground. Past a tall fence the field opened up to a lush green where the brook turned into a river. She jumped the fence and he chased her through the tall grass, up a dirt road, through some woods and someone's yard where she fell to her back in the moist, thick growth and laughed at the sky. He stood at a distance and watched her until she sat up and looked at him. He walked over and sat next to her. They stayed there, watching each other and an old man stepping out of a shack to feed his chickens across the river.

"This is not paralysis, by any means, but a kind of shock"

"the intention of being suspended" "or lying dormant"

"an adhesion"

"an appearance"

"something not completeley palatable"

"like earth and dirt"

"the sweetness and the ash"

thin layers of silt and mud like quicksilver joining
and splitting plains lined by rows of stranded rocks
ancient shorelines jutting out into the uneven retreat
of glacial ice a kind of paradise of Walnut or Cedar
or Chestnut "& stones to strike fire" "fish and fur,
oaken ship timbers, spars and masts of white pine,
iron made from ore raked from the floors of coal
bogs" "the Wildernesse" "a cleere resemblance of
this world" kernels of corn in the ear of a crow

"here were the flowers"

"prairies by the sea"

"the music, as of old"

"set like jewels in the green expanse"

He rocked back and forth gently in the seat, bundled up in a coat not thick enough, the collar not high enough to shield the draft against his neck that whistled through the windlacing, chipped and cracked in places from dry rot. The roads curved dark and came to one lane covered bridges, perfect S and U turns. He followed smaller rivers until they ended then found the source of them and remained in pursuit, crossing and re-crossing at bridges that looked the longest. The radio crackled then got clear again as he veered in and out of towns whose houses clung to the sides of the mountains, like the road, a ribbon that had been snipped out of the deep rooted rock and growth. Around a curve he came close to hitting two horses pulling a wagon filled with people. The tires gripped and skidded but he got by them and saw their black figures in the rear view mirror, their arms as they pulled at the reins and the heads of the startled horses whose frothing white teeth gripped their bits and swung a white arc in the sky as their masters faded back into the black earth. He thought of finding her, if only as a way of explaining that look in her eyes when she stepped off the bus and walked across the lot, her legs unsure of her body's weight. He stayed out of the sun watching her until she got in the shadow of a dolly filled with luggage in front of a wall of coin lockers. His eyes must have been wilder, under the moon in the mist, when he had called after her, begging. He awoke to a dull thud, followed by a yelp, and cleared his eyes to see a small brown dog chased by a bigger grey one. The sun hadn't yet cleared the top of the mountain, the purple drawing slowly to reveal orange then yellow with china blue behind it. Hadn't he been across the street, on the steps of an abandoned building, waiting? They had all walked down past the pier, past the boats loading and unloading, getting fuel and checking their oil, to the rocks and across the rocks to the end of the jetty. They sat there and watched a trawler steam through toward the docks. Two men stood on deck, each with a foot on the railing. They waved as the gulls dove and pecked at whatever bait was left on the nets. Would she remember telling him how she had spent the day at the quarries, in the cold deep water, her clothes lying in the moss as she dove off the sides and slid across the sharp black rocks, her body moist on the edge of the soft, damp soil, the leaves above caressed by the breeze? Continuing across the border, he took that desolate stretch of road north: squat wire fences with grey posts and faded signs on rusted mounts, a vast intractable land under an unchanging sky. He drove by what he knew must be the house, slow wide hills, then flat for a stretch, all grey, the houses weathered grey, the shingles tight and straight. He pulled off to the dirt shoulder and left it there, the faded lines disappearing in the distance. He got to the short path leading to the house and heard a screen door creak as a woman wearing a white cotton dress emerged from the shadow. Before he said anything, she started: "You have just missed her, we tried to call, the one that answered said you had left. She's gone to meet her father, my husband drove her." He watched her small lips, her handsome face below her grey hair, the lines belonging there. He nodded, as the voice came back to him again, through the static, after all the waiting: "Ten, twelve, fifteen times, my stomach, my back, my legs, my arms. It was complicated. Believe me I tried." He imagined her lying on the sidewalk in a pool of blood soaked black into the cement. The knife was found in a trash can. He thanked her again and said goodbye, hearing the door snap back and her steps fade through the hall of the empty house. Listening to their echo, he turned to look at the vast flat land below the thick grey sky.

unite yourselves with us in size and grandeur
seek the plentiful harbor diligently collect
history written in bone examine these earliest
artifacts the first examples the last vestiges
keep the continent from being blank a place
of imprisonment dumb with the question
four sevenths of agricultural production
taken over corn carried on their backs
seventy miles one of the first desparate
years as a gift long before anyone assumed
we made a mistake in trying to bear witness
all this wonder all this newness the body
wrapped in bark the vessel polished with the
tooth of a beaver a gift from the departed
smoked in a lobster claw alders lichen
bloodroot and sumac how we played
compelled and blind our claim no emptier
than questions of industry and idleness
survivors of our expectation the law of the
land recollected carefully in the hollow the
ambition to come to meaning before inquiry
the itinerant faces of defeated ancesters crop
up again adrift think of their names like our
hands shadows at the bottom of the sea

"Something like soul, that you are witness to, that you remember, by experience, by surfaces":

"some great great wound" "in the whole body"

"so unwieldy, so completely irretrievable"

                                        "no one dares" "operate"

"Bleecker Street was a lane lined with blackberry bushes, and in the berry season was a great place for picnics from far and near. It was also a good region for snipe shooting, and also for hunting rabbits. But by now you would have hardly recognized the place. For the city had grown up into it."

how long ago we walked unwinding the jewels there
on the meadow of yellow flowers on the meadow of
blue flowers under the growing corn we used to sit
the blue flowers woven over the yellow ones the place
which is called black spot with life the place which is
called blue spot with life the white circle in the sand
this gold the emblems these waters claim your boat
the irises you grasp a deceit you cannot name now
this tension shattering the sacred places the
slaughter we live by trying to remember
as rocks are ground to powder
and made into blocks

"the ghost of the pain"

"*is* the circle of wild horses"

"The price of freedom isn't cheap," the sergeant said. "People could at least invest a little time."

"They are old men now, drifting into town in their boots, blue jeans and silver buckles. Like other aging veterans, they meet once a month on Saturday mornings for a blend of poignant and prosaic duties: planning parades, disbursing money for the funeral expenses of one old comrade and a small scholarship for the son of another and reviewing the coffee budget, $21.69 this month. But more than fifty years ago, the fifteen men in the Chamber of Commerce hall by the railroad tracks fought fiercely for the flag of a country that had given their people nothing but grief. And the embroidery on the battered red and yellow caps covering their grizzled heads and tanned faces proclaims their proud name"

a dream muffled and dumb memories of the hanging
gardens the bird part prophecy part longing the waters
sure the stones and trees insensible their leaves of green
of red of yellow things long since fled the hunter and
the deer the posture that we give the dead a painted bowl
arrows with a head of stone painted chief and painted spear
this charm my garments the city where I hope to dwell like
trash not silk the streets transparent gold imprisoned
lightning silent lips astride the market-place of war where
death and glory meet ancient rage and old despair their
beauty and their strength their parts their ports their pomp
call back some time now past the fatal rhythm of their tread
your own rehearsal revisiting the congregation like wasted
strangers as if they were alive without record in their
own language speaking some simple word of treasure
next time when all of these are gone

"when I thought of all this paraphernalia
of American Democracy behind me

and the project of liberty before me":

"slavery with its Democratic whips—

its Republican chains—

                            its evangelical blood-hounds"

"experienced in the knowledge"

"punctual in measuring"

"Let them feed on this ground"

"observant of these heavenly lights"

"like an unaccustomed ghost"

"That starts,"

"surprised,"

"to stumble over graves,"

"the names of people once numerous"

"A vessel carried away a great number of our surprised Indians, in the times of our wars, to sell them for slaves, but the nations, wither she went, would not buy them. Finally, she left them at Tangier; there they may be, so many as live, or are born there. An Englishman, a mason, came thence to Boston, he told me they desired I would use some means for their return home. I know not what to do in it; but now it is in my heart to move your honour, so to mediate, that they may have leave to go home, either from thence hither, or from thence to England, and so to get home"

do not feel badly because you have lost
sight of this daylight no matter how hard
I try nothing happens today to you alone
those who have reached the place where
death stands waiting have not pointed out
a way to circumvent it I myself grieve when
I look back there into the past it is enough
to make anyone ponder now here at last
we are ready to end this when you start
to leave you must not think back
with regret you always return
garment of brightness
wilderness
in the midst
of plenty

"farewell bright moment,

lingering sun":

"this heart"

"will never"

"awaken"

5.

night of unity

it had long been the position of the United States that
the warring parties could work out their own alliances

> National Security Advisor Anthony Lake
> to Ambassador of Bosnia-Hercegovina
> to the United States Sven Alkalaj
> November 30, 1994

> *Rise, shining martyrs*
> *over the multitudes*
> *for the season of migration*
> *between earth and heaven*

> John Wieners

we swam the submerged body all the way to the boat

before hoisting it on deck. We were fully dressed

Struck by her wisdom and intelligence, the king carries on
long conversations with her—about God, politics, love,
family, loyalty, betrayal and the will of the people. Along
the way he reveals his insecurities. He wonders whether
people will honor or desecrate his corpse after he dies.

"At work in both uprisings were the same material costs, the same first causes. Little had really changed in the intervening years. The same regency governed in the old manner, that is, as deemed fit, through the same narrow ring of privileged oligarchs, under the same thin pretense of constitutional politics. On occasion, as before, the parties, the publicists, the colleges, drew a breath. The regime had to concede that much to preserve itself. But, as before, the freedoms hesitantly granted were hurriedly snatched back, or allowed only in form and frustrated in practice. Those of the lower-classes, of the mud huts, still lived in squalor, ate polluted food and drudged long hours at impossible wages."

"from the same standpoint, the notion 'class' demands or presupposes the notion 'inequality,' and therefore implies at least one other class— the 'inequality' being basically with respect to 'property.'"

"But this does not mean that it is, therefore, merely an intellectual category, that is, something foisted on reality by the mind. The members of a class may not be class-conscious in their behavior, but their behavior could nonetheless be class-conditioned."

"The book is kind of a dirge.

The king is talking about his death.

Everytime I read the book I feel for the king."

"what is interesting and appealing to me is how you slow
down the pace, how you use quotations as a model of
reflection, a slow motion historical record, weighted and
measured, where the isolated citations act as characters.
They are cool and concise as if part of the written record.
At the same time, they are ethereal, as if outside the
record. As if they were/are from the warring factions—
past, present and future—come to address us about
the history they've witnessed."

"We stick with the plan," Mr. Thomas said. "We insist that the map be accepted." He added that "rumors" about the plan's being changed were untrue.

"One former director said gleaning facts from the avalanche of information was like trying to take a drink of water from a fire hose."

The cover of the novel says only that it is "by its author."

"The same old presumption, that a human supposition of itself, 'language,' may be employed to tell words what they may or may not be, do, and so on. So, e.g., what of the life of words and the possible experience of words once 'language' has argued its system of same as limit of same. Which I am persuaded is coeval with the 'innovation' of writing itself, systems thereof—i.e. what was written in being more or less the familiar argument of itself as all, and what one knows had to be written out, and had to be written out for ideological reasons. Indeed, what was written in is what's called the book, and thus the revered perspective of cosmos as book, and any manifest of same as text, to be read... For ex., one term from the beginning written in is property; one term written out, except as she consent to serve it, is woman. Meaning all the actual agency of woman—i.e. what I take to have been a vast, particular knowledge not simply of herself, but of all of cosmos that falls to woman by 'natural' affinity to 'understand.' What I am clumsily getting at is that the 'civilized' in each of its signature terms does stem from a single—to me unaccountable—ambition to control (in every possible sense, including cyberspace... cyber = as I remember it, in Greek, the helmsman, the steerer...) the experience of human being as the latter is understood to be at the centrality of what's meant by 'life on earth.' Which it is not, and which asininity we are presently harvesting in every single dimension of our existences and so are all other creatures of earthly and not-so-earthly existence also being obliged to harvest that oafish ideological lie."

One night, while returning to her cottage from the king's palace, Zabibah is gagged and dragged into a forest where she is raped by a man who conceals his identity. He turns out to be her estranged husband. Afterward, Zabibah says to herself, "Rape is the most serious of crimes, whether it is a man raping a woman or invading armies raping the homeland." The enraged king vows revenge by opening a war "that will not end until victory or death." During the ensuing battle against the husband and his supporters, Zabibah is killed. Her husband, who is killed the same day, is buried beside her so that the people can throw stones on his grave to desecrate it on the anniversary of his death.

"It was just eight years after the end of World War II, which left American journalists with a sense of national interest framed by six years of confrontation between the Allies and the Axis. The front pages of Western newspapers were dominated by articles about the new global confrontation with the Soviet Union, about Moscow's prowess in developing nuclear weapons and about Congressional allegations of 'Red' influences in Washington."

"tribes, guilds and mystic orders lost cohesion or
disintegrated; vast masses of people moved from
the country and provincial towns to the big cities
to enroll in the new army, bureaucracy, or police
force, or to find employment in the new businesses
that supplied the needs of these institutions, or to
swell the ranks of the unskilled laborers and
noticeably depress their earnings; old ties, loyalties,
and concepts were undermined, eroded, or swept away."

"lost to history,"

"the subject of fierce debate"

the operation's success was mostly a matter of chance

One by one, participants retired or died without revealing key details, and the agency said a number of records of the operation—its first succesful overthrow of a foreign government, had been destroyed.

"I wanted to let Freedman know that I knew there had been involvement in the coup, but that I hadn't written about it," he said. "I expected him to say, 'Jump on that story.' But there was no response."

"He makes the proper sacrifices, and advances

to the scales of justice. There he sees his own

heart weighed against the ostrich-feather of Truth."

"Let this cave be Egypt"

the sentence, if this throne has a language:

kinetoscope reels the x-ray the wireless telegraph the mystery of radium

`

"dazzling as the wheels of Ezekiel"

"the sword like a stream of light

the moth that burns its wings in the lamp"

"he says there is no substitute for time,

the shadow it throws upon the screen"

"it is a crude mind that would insist these
appearances are not real, that the eye does
not see them when all eyes behold them"

"they go to film after film till the whole world

seems to turn on a reel"

"the reel now before us"

"survives the shrinking

and the warping"

"THE CHAPTERS ON COMING FORTH BY DAY"

"mysterious fourth dimension of its grace and glory"

"Half lies, half truths," the writer took "poetic license."
 "Poetic license," he says, "drives me crazy."

"The field was filled with white specks and from
a distance, they looked like mushrooms but when
you moved up closer, you realized they were all skulls."

if we want to talk

about *things*:

I left my mattress

I left my mattress cover

I left my pillow

I left my plate and my cup

I left the clothing that I wore

I left everything and nothing

"these people down here, this is like an echo chamber, it's an echo chamber that resonates with the testimony of the living witnesses—and these people, these dead people are telling us the same story that the living witnesses have told us" many people march toward the strange glorifying eye of

the camera growing larger filling the entire field of

vision disappearing when they are almost upon us

imagine a production that would chronicle the promise

"as a method of keeping the story from ending"

"with the white glare of the empty screen":

"darkness"

"on which we can paint" "the feeling of return":

"THE QUESTION OF OUR DEPARTURE"

August 2, 2001, the day General Radislav Krstić was convicted of genocide and sentenced to forty-six years by the International Criminal Tribunal in the Hague for his role in the massacre of some 7,000 people at Srebrenica

a conversation

Benjamin Hollander: We've read each other's work over the years, I've been involved in reading and commenting on this book while it was in manuscript, we've discussed it, and we've discussed how people might respond to it. First, tell me, how did you arrive at writing *from the warring factions*? I'm interested in what, in particular, moved it from head to page, but, more importantly—and as perhaps part of a continuum with your previous work as a poet, translator, scholar, and journalist—how was the moment ripe for this particular book?

Ammiel Alcalay: I'm not quite sure how all this will get defined historically, but it seems to me that numerous poetry movements now in the forefront have attracted people who, in some sense, are trying to lose themselves. Or at least blur the boundaries of their own biographies, particularly in terms of class or cultural background. What then happens is that people who are not part of the dominant scene or "white" in that sense, people who have not been educated in elite institutions, are allowed to have biographies because this, somehow, makes them "authentic." Although it is changing, we still have this underlying rift between what gets represented as formally "sophisticated" and often de-personalized work on the one hand and emotionally "genuine" and personal, but formally "naïve," work on the other. I think this is a significantly different frame of mind than previous generations —those, for example, we've lumped under the rubric of "New American" poets. This only seems to be getting worse as professionalization and specialization proceed apace. So a lot of my work as a scholar, journalist, translator, and teacher has been to open up space for work that, on a surface level, might seem "conventional" or "merely" personal, but which actually represents radical forms of consciousness and engagement with historical circumstances. We haven't really come up with aesthetic or theoretical terms to adequately deal with this kind of writing or with the impact such writing can have on more formally adventurous work.

Beyond this dichotomy, there is an even more insidious syndrome that I find on the social level which I think is related: too many writers lead incredibly segregated lives, with only other writers as friends; they find it hard to relate to people out of their guild. This is true for most vocations in the United States, and it is very different from what goes on in other parts of the world. A lot of the issues I am concerned with relate to this difference, particularly when one thinks about who the work is directed to or how it might have some effect on a culture or society. Some of the other literary social scenes I am familiar with, in ex-Yugoslavia or the Middle East, are far less exclusive. This makes writers focus their attention on a wider spectrum of things and has an impact on aesthetic or poetic decisions.

Writing and form in the United States, while incredibly rich and unique, are only beginning to grapple with the historical burdens of being part of the world, figuring out why the world is structured the way it is. It is hard to think, for example, of passages that resonate with the absolute particularity and timelessness of the Palestinian Mahmoud Darwish, as he writes about himself as "the poet" retracing the routes of his exile, searching not for "the homeland" but for "the boy that used to be in him, whom he had left behind some place and forgotten." I can think of many writers whose first reaction to such a passage might be that it is "sentimental." But if you know something about the poet's personal history, about the historical circumstances of the people he is a part of, and about the time this text refers to, the passage is both revolutionary and lacerating. It is revolutionary in the sense that it opens up personal history in a tradition of writing that has largely concerned itself with the fate of a people; it is lacerating in that it tears open the loneliness and emotional suppression so often woven into a national history.

In addition to the experience of exile found in Darwish, which can still be assimilated in a post-modern American literary context, we need to go further and look at writers who have undergone unimaginable suffering and humiliation as political prisoners, like the Moroccan poet Abdellatif Laabi or the Syrian poet Faraj Bayraqdar. In the infamous Tadmor prison in Syria, Bayraqdar wrote poems on cigarette papers with ink invented from tea and onion leaves, using wood splinters as a pen. As a result, his use of words like "captivity" and "freedom" resonate in ways we can barely imagine. Some contemporary American poets may align themselves aesthetically to a Mandelstam, but this aligment is culturally and politically sanctioned and obfuscates the fact that the world is filled with "Mandelstams" that have fallen through the cracks of American imperial interests. That is why, when writing like this enters not only my frame of consciousness but my being, I want to know how to situate myself, in my own language, at my own moment. I find myself involved in figuring out the different kinds of resonance writing can have—writing that has a collective, historical resonance and writing that resonates back in on itself, as so much American writing does, to tap our isolation. This makes history crucial for me at all levels, from the personal and familial to the collective.

One's biography becomes very much part of the story. In my own case, I spent about eight years in Jerusalem, the first time from 1978 to 1980, the second time from 1984 until the end of 1989. Luckily, I didn't go with the usual baggage American Jews carry. I had no formal Jewish education; my sense of being a Jew came from my extended family which, by American standards, was pretty eccentric. Since we were Sephardic (meaning our origins were in 15th century Spain and, most likely, in Iraq some three or four hundred years earlier, in the wave of immigration to the West), we didn't fit into any of the existing categories. There were many languages spoken in my family—mainly Serbian and Italian, but also Ladino, French, Greek, German and a little Turkish—and many stories were told by parents, grandparents, aunts, and uncles with no organized or institutionally sanctioned narrative. It was all a puzzle I had to piece together. Since I was aware and active during turbulent political times—the mass protests against the war in Vietnam, schools and universities on strike, cities in turmoil, and so on—when I saw the political situation in Israel, I didn't go through either the partisan fanaticism or disillusionment so many people experience in relation to their expectations about the place. I just fell in with the right people and soon got involved in social and political movements.

One of the reasons I was interested in going to Jerusalem specifically, in addition to studying Arabic and Hebrew, was the lack of resonance between the American context and my background, that of a Sephardic Jew whose family was conscious of their difference. I had a connection through a rabbi I knew in New York, the Hacham Salomon Gaon, originally from Travnik in Bosnia (the same town, ironically, that is part of the history of my wife's family, whom I had just met). He hooked me up with an institution called the Council of the Sephardic Community where I ended up working part-time, as a kind of English secretary and editor. The Council was strangely enveloped in another time, peopled by old Jerusalemites who, along with Hebrew, all spoke Arabic, Ladino, and sometimes Yiddish. They used to publish a cultural magazine and I noticed writers there who were completely different from what was being dished out in the mainstream—it reminded me of seeing America through *Yugen* or the *Black Panther Party* paper as opposed to the *New Yorker*. Listening to them I recognized accents people had been made to feel ashamed of and I began to grasp the scope of ways of life that had gone underground or just been obliterated. It also resonated with the changes I had seen my family go through and resist as immigrants in the United States.

Later I got to know members of the Israeli Black Panthers, the mizrahi social justice movement made up of people Golda Meir had once called "not very nice boys." I soon found out that most of the Jews in prison in Israel had names like mine, names like Alfassi, Algazi or Abulafia, the very names of great thinkers and poets whose books you couldn't find amongst the "cultured and enlightened" mainstream Ashkenazi intellectuals. I got to know younger people involved in forming new social and cultural movements who quickly became, and remain to this day, my contemporaries, friends I look to for instruction and sustenance. This was a period of great social upheaval in Israel —the old order of the Labor Party was swept away by the then opposition Likud Party, led by Menahem Begin. All kinds of skeletons were coming out of various closets and the issue of racism against mizrahim—Jews with origins in the Arab and non-European world—and class difference between Ashkenazi and Sephardi / mizrahi Jews was everywhere. Things were very raw, and this was reflected in music, writing, and art. The correlations between aesthetic blindness or consciousness and social / political blindness or consciousness were evident everywhere you looked.

Through my study of Arabic and involvement with an odd "interfaith" group, I got to know many Palestinians, and began to learn about their situation and history. As an American in Israeli society with a Sephardic consciousness and an awareness of the Palestinian perspective, I found myself in a unique position. I could pass for white and was privy to all kinds of racist behavior that people couldn't imagine I would object to. This experience was formative for me, and it reinscribed things that I was certainly aware of growing up in the United States but which were only driven home for me by being in Israel / Palestine. And it was through the mizrahi and Palestinian activists and artists that I befriended—through the work they produced and the movements they created—that I began to grasp the true sequence of cultural permission and transmission in the formation of knowledge as a collective endeavor, rather than the way we are usually taught such things proceed—through acts of singular perseverance or genius.

The second period in Jerusalem was even more intense: I was working on what would become the books *After Jews & Arabs* as well as *Keys to the Garden*, while continuing my involvement in both mizrahi and Palestinian movements. I was one of the original members of a group called East for Peace, a group combatting stereotypes against mizrahi Jews and linking issues of social justice to the Palestinian issue, something the mainstream Israeli left had never done. I was doing a research project on the political attitudes of Arabic-speaking Jews involving extensive interviews and oral histories. It was published in French and Arabic and had quite an effect, leading to illegal meetings with the PLO during the period when Israel had banned any meetings with them. My work with mizrahi writers eventually led to *Keys to the Garden*; this enabled me to better understand the mechanisms of racist exclusion in the academy, cultural venues, the media, and publishing. I was also involved in the Committee Confronting the Iron Fist, a group of Palestinians (including the late Faisal Husseini), Israelis and foreigners who were trying to stretch the borders of permissible protest and raise awareness about the effects of the military occupation. There were dozens of other groups that we were involved in; there was also work for local and international organizations on the use of torture and the conditions of political prisoners. Then came the huge prisoner exchange when all the Palestinians emerged from years of Israeli incarceration with their doctorates and post-docs in revolution—and after that the first intifada began in 1987. From this vantage point, those were incredibly hopeful years: more and more people began to recognize the courage and audacity of such a massive popular uprising. There was a sense that, at least on a local level, real change was in the making, one that might affect the order of things. It was moving and enlightening to be involved in such a process, and it continues to inform what I do and how I think about things. Life there, oddly, was much less segregated—writers and artists that I knew never made too big of a deal about what they did outside of just regular human activity. Or maybe it was the other way around—art or writing could be seen as just another part of regular activity.

Throughout this period, and later as well, I spent quite a bit of time in ex-Yugoslavia, with those parts of my family that stayed, and with my in-laws who had both fought with the Partisans during the Second World War. This gave me a unique perspective on the country my parents came from, an experience that not many first generation Americans have had. Not long after coming back to New York, the Gulf War began and I had a distinct and awful sense that huge and powerful forces were coming into play in order to, indeed, dictate a new world order, one that is now with us in an even more unspeakably insidious, pervasive, and suffocating form.

I give prominence to all these apparently external events because they were an inseparable part of the life I was engaged in and, as such, had absolute repercussions on the forms and direction my writing took. Doing book reviews for large circulation newspapers, thinking about language for public debate or political leaflets, doing court transcripts of political prisoners, or translating testimonies of children who had been tortured—these were not discrete activities that I could check at the door marked "art." I tried to capture the horror, discovery, defiance, and humanity of those years in Jerusalem in *the cairo notebooks*, published in 1993 but mostly completed, I think, sometime in 1991. I wanted to get down as much as I could, but the sense remained with me that I was writing a message in a bottle, something to be retrieved, something to be deciphered and interpreted later on. In that book, I not only used documentary materials, I pillaged my own writing, some of it dating back to the 1970s. I felt that it was important not to jettison parts of other, older selves, but to bring them along for the ride into this new world I now inhabited and which had become an integral part of me. Paradoxically, by hanging on to those older selves in new contexts, one makes an example out of one-self and removes the work from the trappings of ideology that surround the individual. I could enact and re-enact this movement through history, going back in time in a person-al way but also interrogating the materials of political, cul-tural, and human encounters rooted in specific places and times. I could see, for example, that experiences I had de-monstrating against the bombing of Cambodia in high school (my brother led a strike that shut down the school), or the many hours I spent talking to Black Panthers selling the party paper on the streets of Cambridge or Boston, were things I carried with me to Palestine and Israel, sources I drew on as I encountered and attempted to represent con-flicts there. Even as I was working on *the cairo notebooks*, and certainly when it was finished, I had the sense of it as something I call "a compressed novel," with the further sense that it was part of a much larger, ongoing work.

By relating all these activities, I am, in a sense, taking the easy way out and pointing to the more obvious connections between experiences and how they enter the work. The deeper question, and the one that is more difficult to get a handle on, has to do with how this consciousness of politi-cal realities entered my poetry, how it came to matter in the work closest to me. I was following the "poetry wars" in the United States through little mags when I was in Jerusalem and, while I was very taken with many of the ideas debated, the concept of intellectual work in the situations of urgency I was involved in was both more tangible and, in many ways, more theoretically encompassing—so many other factors embedded in real historical time and human motivation were at work. During the "Camps War" in Lebanon, for instance, we did vigils at the al-Hakawati theater in East Jerusalem. A number of the actors had relatives caught in a situation where local religious authorities had given residents permission to eat human flesh because of starvation caused by an absolute siege. Besides the emotions of the people involved, the director had to figure out ways to incorporate this reality into the possibility of the performance. It boils down to an almost ancient view of things—art shouldn't primarily be about beauty but about pain and suffering. At the same time, one has to use positions of privilege in the structure of this society to illustrate how one can give up those privileges voluntarily, or put them in the service of things other than self-promotion. I find it deeply disturbing, for example, that you can read a lot of innovative poetry from the last decade without even getting a hint that two genocides took place in the world. I can't think of an American poem marking the age the way Charles Olson's 1946 poem "La Préface" did, with the lines: "'My name is NO RACE' address / Buchenwald new Altamira cave," and "We are born not of the buried but these unburied dead."

Benjamin Hollander: How would you hope that a reader not familiar with your work—or, for that matter, not as involved with reading poetry in general—might enter the writing? Or, put another way: where would you like this reader's conversation with you to go, once someone has read *from the warring factions*?

Ammiel Alcalay: I mentioned "professionalization" before. I would like to take that further: it seems to me that life has become standardized in this country, that there is much less room left than when I was growing up. Time is more direct-ed, particularly if you're middle-class, and the mass media has managed to encase experiences in a stock set of imagery that, almost literally, envelops experience. There are less chances to encounter eccentric people, less places of idle-ness, places where conversations can take place. There is a big difference between a Barnes & Noble and the kinds of bookstores I used to hang out at as a teenager in Boston, like the Grolier or the Temple Bar. I was somewhat of a delinquent and didn't find school very useful. There were periods when I divided my time between the streets, where a lot was happening, movies, a garage where I worked, pool halls, and bookstores. The Grolier was then owned by the legendary Gordon Cairnie, and he even encouraged me to skip school! It was quite something to be a teenager and see Conrad Aiken step out of his apartment above the shop in the morning, to meet the likes of Denise Levertov, Allen Ginsberg, Robert Creeley, Gary Snyder, John Wieners, and so many others. There was a very relaxed, kind of disheveled atmosphere there, with papers and books piled on the couch. The Temple Bar owned by the O'Neil brothers was absolutely uncorked, and I felt completely at home there as well. I want the text to reflect that kind of eccentric space, to strive against "professionalization," to challenge and invite readers into a world where you can always know more, but where what you know—whatever that may be—can still serve you well.

The interesting thing is that I was exposed to this diver-sity of worlds, the old worlds and the new worlds, through my family and the connections my parents made when they came to the United States. They had fled Yugoslavia in 1941 and ended up in Italy where they were on the run, impris-oned at various times but also rescued by Italians. They re-mained in Rome until 1951 and it was there that my father, a painter, had his first exhibits. Through an Italian connection that I believe had something to do with the sculptor and artist Corrado Cagli, they were put in contact with the artists' community in Gloucester that included Charles Olson, Vincent Ferrini, and Mary Shore, all of whom became close family friends. I have very vivid memories of Olson, of playing badminton with him in the front yard of the Benjamin Tarr House, a place we rented for a few summers, and then of later visits from Boston to his place on Fort Square, where there would be penny candy from the general store waiting. I remember my outrage when I heard that a well-known bookseller had gone to see him on his death bed in the hospital to have him sign books. I wrote a potentially libelous letter to this person who was ready to sue me until he realized I was only fourteen! I also remember Olson's funeral vividly, right after the funeral of Jack Kerouac, whom I had already started reading. I was reading voraciously and began writing. American art and poetry and music were very real to me, I grew up with them and around them. One summer I became good friends with someone from New York and began to go there during school vacations and in the summer. I got to see Slug's and the Five Spot, where I heard Cecil Taylor, Ornette Coleman, and so many other great musicians. I would go sit on the steps for the last show at the Village Vanguard, and I heard all kinds of greats there too—Art Pepper, Dexter Gordon, and so on. I got to know various painters, Hugo Weber, for instance, for whom Kerouac had written that great piece "An Imaginary Portrait of Ulysses S. Grant / Edgar Allen Poe," based on one of Hugo's paintings. Back home I commandeered larger and larger parts of my parents' library, especially the little magazines: *Black Mountain Review*, *Evergreen*, *Kulchur*, *Yugen*, *Floating Bear*, all kinds of things. For me, New American poetry was like baseball cards—I not only knew who the starters were, I also knew who the second and even third stringers were. I wrote to everybody—I remember writing to Ginsberg, asking what could be done to bring Kerouac's books back into print. He answered with a postcard, explaining the difficulties. I wrote Diane di Prima about *Floating Bear* and *Yugen*, and she answered in great detail, in a long letter. My first extensive correspondence was with Vincent Ferrini. I would send Vincent my poems and he would shoot these great letters off to me, the same day! So I've always had a very profound and personal sense of the intricacy in networks of transmission and tradition, of how far the really important things are from what *appears* to matter.

The whole New England thing was close to me—Lowell, Gloucester, the Boston that the sadly departed John Wieners describes and which I was lucky enough to still have a taste of before it was almost completely destroyed. In the preface to *Transmutations* by Steve Jonas, whom I met before he died in 1970 (the same year as Olson), John wrote: "They have torn down the West End, they have torn down Scollay Square, they have torn down nearly all of Copley Square, erecting insurance companies, parking lots and underground garages in their place. As a center, they have placed urban restaurants, made out of plate glass and neon signs. Renewal they call it. Gone the elegant, old hotels, basement cafeterias, underground jazz cellars, and strip atheneum. All night movies, the Silver Dollar at the corner of Boylston and Essex are dark while Nedicks shines on. Old haunts of these poems, they become bombs to blow up in the face of the future, they have become the future itself: BLAST; in the face of emblems of the past we live by." All of this became clear to me later as I got to know people from Baghdad or Marrakesh living in Israeli slums, as I saw bulldozers clear olive groves and Palestinians confined to reservation-like conditions.

I continued my involvement in the writing scene through the late 1970s by studying with Toby Olson and then Gilbert Sorrentino in New York. I learned an enormous amount from Sorrentino, and my critical work is still indebted to his clarity and sense of judgment; he urged me to study languages and I began taking classes in Latin and Ancient Greek at City College. I was more than somewhat removed from the late 1970s until almost the mid 1990s. As I said, eight of those years were spent outside the country and, even though I followed the writing through magazines, I didn't have that intimate sense of who people are that one has when one is in the middle of it. So for me, coming back to the United States in 1990 meant engaging in a long process of reorienting my own poetic, personal, and collective cultural history. I went to readings, of course, mainly at the Ear Inn and the St. Marks Poetry Project, and reconnected with a lot of people. Finding Gil Ott was crucial—he published my "Understanding Revolution" in *Paper Air*, and then *the cairo notebooks* with Singing Horse Press. This presented challenges to many on the scene because of the issues I was dealing with: torture, imprisonment, military occupation, and so on. Following the poetry wars of the 1980s from Jerusalem, I put that debate to very different use because of my background, where I was coming from, and my experience abroad. My re-entry here involved a close identification with people one or several generations older than me; I started to get to know people I had been reading for years, in some cases since I was a teenager, but had never met or met only briefly at a younger age. This is an ongoing, exciting process, letting me repossess the instincts of my early readings, to reconfirm those early allegiances and intimacies, to find and lose myself in them again. I would mention, as examples, Robert Creeley, Etel Adnan, Gerrit Lansing, Duncan McNaughton, David Meltzer, Jerry Rothenberg, the late Armand Schwerner, Robin Blaser, Jack Hirschman, Fanny Howe, Anne Waldman, and Joanne Kyger, among others.

All of this came to a head when, just as the Gulf War ended, the new Balkan wars began. Having family and friends in ex-Yugoslavia, and knowing the language, put me close to another externalized but personal series of historical events. This was an urgent period of work, translating and trying to open up space for Bosnian voices. I did things from both ends—from small press projects that were absolutely essential, to mass media work, for *Time*, *The New York Times*, the *Village Voice,* and so on. Before the war broke out, I was working on a special issue of a magazine called *Lusitania* with a friend, the Palestinian artist and translator Kamal Boulatta. It originally was meant to be dedicated to the 500th year of the expulsion of Jews and Arabs from Spain, examined from the perspective of the conflict between Israelis and Palestinians. It was clear, however, that Bosnia was really the new Andalusia, and it was under attack. Kamal left the country after the Gulf War so I put together a bilingual Bosnian / English issue dedicated to Sarajevo, with the unwavering support of publisher and cartoonist Martim Avillez. It was the first thing to come out in the States of its kind on Bosnia, with faxes that I got from villages that had been overrun, reports from Bosnian journalists, selections from the *Witnesses of Existence* art exhibit that we eventually helped bring to New York from Sarajevo, selections from classic, pre-modern Bosnian writers, and so on. In addition, I asked writers whose work meant something to me to contribute pieces that didn't necessarily have anything to do with Bosnia—Adonis, Juan Goytisolo, Etel Adnan, Juan Felipe Herrera, Naomi Shihab Nye, the late Jacques Hassoun, Jimmie Durham, Alexis De Veaux, and others. It was a chance to really explore my developing aesthetic. This too became a kind of challenge to the existing literary scene, particularly given the almost apartheid-like criteria of anthologies, with "experimentalists" on one side and "ethnics" on the other. Add to this the fact that we were in the middle of witnessing a televised genocide. Greil Marcus picked the issue as one of his Top Ten of 1993 in

Artforum, and that helped open up more space. I understood that one could hack away at constraints from both ends.

While I had immersed myself in the roles you mention—scholar, teacher, journalist, poet, critic, activist—regarding the Middle East, it was through my involvement in Bosnia that I began to more clearly define and examine these roles and what they meant to me here, in relation to a public, or a diversity of publics. Interestingly enough, coming to California fairly regularly was essential to all of this. I had spent time in San Francisco in the mid 1970s—I was working at an auto body shop someplace on Howard Street, a whole area, in fact, that isn't even there anymore. When I came in 1994, students in Near Eastern Studies at Berkeley had pressured the department to invite me; I did a reading at Small Press Traffic with Juan Felipe Herrera, and another at City Lights. It was the first time for me that my audiences began to converge—poets were picking up on my Middle East work, and Middle East people were looking at my poetry. Etel Adnan, the Lebanese writer and artist, was a crucial conduit for this. I started to connect with people I had never met but whose work and activities I had followed from Jerusalem—Norma Cole, Laura Moriarty, Steve Dickison, Michael Palmer, and so many others. That's when I made the initial connection to everyone at City Lights and Bob Sharrard, the editor I've worked with so closely on numerous projects. I can't overemphasize how important this was, and remains, for me. Altogether, the West Coast has provided a more receptive space for my work, not just in the Bay Area but in Vancouver, Seattle, and places like Beyond Baroque in Los Angeles. This isn't surprising, given the inordinate pressures from mainstream intellectuals in New York to evade the US relationship to the Middle East and alternative versions of Jewish history. I remember reading Kenneth Rexroth's pieces on the provinciality of New York's literary culture and I've been finding more and more truth in it over the years.

Having developed a network of poets and writers of different generations whose work matters to me here, in this country, I find myself in a paradoxical position—as this milieu becomes more a part of my internal landscape, I also feel a certain distance from it. Recently I've found it almost uncomfortable to not be around people involved in, and conscious of, things related to the Middle East. Luckily, in the past five or so years, a nucleus of writers, artists, filmmakers, scholars, students, and activists has developed in New York. One doesn't feel nearly so isolated, especially when there is a crisis and one must contend with the barrage of ignorant, racist misinformation that our mass media consists of. I also get much of my energy and sustenance from people I'm in close or sporadic touch with around the world, in Beirut, Tel Aviv, Sarajevo, and other places. There is a level of urgency that is absent, for the most part, from the American poetic or intellectual landscape, tainted as it is by complacency, plain laziness, and cowardice. As I put it in *Memories of Our Future* (1999), "the insularity of American cultural life presents very real political problems and writers have a crucial role to play in disturbing this deadly slumber." Addressing this has refined my allegiances. Many of the responses (or lack of responses) following the events of September 11th further confirmed the distance I feel from so much of what goes on here in the name of "art" or "culture."

Being a writer entails responsibility, first to yourself and the language you are using but then, beyond that, to disrupt accepted patterns of seeing things, to get people to pay attention to things in the world that matter. It means taking risks outside the circumscribed risk-taking not only allowed but promoted within a controlled, even self-policed "avant-garde." These risks can be political, emotional, even formal. For some, writing conventional narratives might constitute risk-taking. For others, taking a political stand, and making it public, may put privileges at risk. I am sure that some of my public positions have cut me off from opportunities I'm not even aware of. In the larger scheme of things, this is not such a big deal, but it does place one in a different position regarding dominant assumptions and the powers that be.

I have gotten no solace from seeing just how unprepared so many people who claim to be writers or intellectuals were following September 11th. I think that, given the forces at work in the world now, this gap can only widen. It is quite a pitiful state of affairs; too many people remain blissful in their ignorance and it is, at least partially, because of them that the state of things has gotten as bad as it is. The Palestinian situation, or the sanctions against Iraq, are examples that serve as a kind of litmus test for US double standards in the world; the unwillingness of North American intellectuals or writers to confront these things head on displays a profound point of acquiescence to the accepted order. But putting the onus on something happening far away is also simplistic—such issues must become the means through which we interrogate our own relationships to the dispossessed among us, here. Power abhors a vacuum, and when there is no one ready to stand in and provide a reality check, to interrogate what passes for knowledge and gets translated into policy, then those actively working to advance an agenda can run roughshod over the populace, from the highest levels of government to the decisions editors make in commercial or even small press publishing.

After September 11th, and for several months prior, my political commentaries had only been appearing abroad, primarily in Bosnia and Croatia. While this has been frustrating in one sense, I also find it refreshing. It has given me a kind of freedom not that easily granted in literary or intellectual circles here, enabling me to look at things both clearly and idiosyncratically. It is strange to be publishing regularly abroad in the leading papers of Bosnia (*DANI*) and Croatia

(*Feral Tribune*), doing major interviews for them, even having a regular column for a time.

I wrote, for example, a piece critical of Susan Sontag's acceptance of the 2001 Jerusalem Prize. I specifically wanted to publish it for a Bosnian audience since her interventions there had been truly courageous. In it, I spoke of Sontag's clear understanding of the responsibilities that come with the privilege of public exposure, and how she was able to use that to great advantage to make people aware of the siege of Sarajevo. But by going to accept a prize in Jerusalem, she allowed herself to be fit into a preordained scheme in which the message of freedom was delivered in a divided city, under military occupation. I, among others, was disappointed that she would enter a hall of mirrors, a city that has become a virtual theme park of simulation and constructed history, without knowing in her gut where the real skeletons were hidden. What I found most troubling was that she entered this space of illusion willingly, knowing that *they* knew she would be crucial to Israel's policy of self-legitimation. Now, if she knew that, surely she must have sensed that they could only use such a demonstration as another public media moment to prove, yet again, how liberal and open to criticism they are. At any rate, in a recent interview with Sontag in *DANI*, they quoted me back to her. I was referred to as "a well-known Jewish intellectual," a category I am generally not considered belonging to in the United States. I relate all this to emphasize that this discursive encounter between Sontag and myself could never have occurred in the United States. Here we're playing in different leagues, and the commissioners are out there to make sure that no one switches leagues without paying a price. That is why it is a great advantage for me to have these outlets abroad. I have seen the kind of price in intellectual integrity one pays through the thirst for recognition and power, regardless of the level it comes at.

As I've said in other places, for me, translation and this

kind of public, journalistic activity have always meant stretching the American context to engage with experiences that are not made to fit existing models. I've looked for work that I would like to have seen somebody write here, but they can't, or haven't, or wouldn't be able to because the circumstances for that writing don't yet exist—that is, there hasn't been any kind of collective, historical moment to use as a reference point. Those moments of suffering haven't yet come to our collective consciousness even though they are deeply present in parts of the population that include such suffering in their vocabulary of memory. The decision to translate Semezdin Mehmedinović, for example, has a lot to do with my aesthetic, my sense that work can serve as its own statement and challenge the complacency with which many writers here seem to approach what they do.

Given my background, with in-laws, relatives and friends living under bombardment and siege, the break-up of Yugoslavia was clearly not something just happening in the newspapers or on TV. One could not go on as if nothing was taking place in actuality. In addition to the work that I was involved in as a translator and activist, I collected massive amounts of documentary material during the war, with the idea of eventually using it in some way as part of a text. The more time I spent with this documentary material, the more I realized that the materials that needed to be brought to bear on the events had to be the materials of culture itself, the materials that appear to remove art from life and confuse a certain rarefied aesthetic with the need to testify. When it came to *from the warring factions*, I wanted to place myself as author / narrator, and the text, in a specific time frame—the time in which the war took place and the text was written. So the first poem places the narrator on a specific date, in a specific place, and it ends on a particular date that happened to coincide with the sentencing of one of the generals responsible for the massacre at Srebrenica—

an event at the center of the text but unspoken until the reference to the sentencing at the end of the book. I needed to confound the whole notion of a narrator, or a single self.

At the same time, I was not writing about something that happened "over there." This has always been the problem of sojourns—one does not always look at the ground upon which one, or all of us, is standing. The whole question of American empire, of the obliteration and genocide of native peoples, for example, presented itself as a lens through which other reference had to be filtered. Other empires, Rome in particular, followed from this. And we can talk about the price of empire, but what about the dispossession of those who fought for it, the veterans? Coursing throughout everything is the simple question of transmission—how does memory survive? To what materials do we entrust it? Have we, in the cinematic and digital age, renounced claims to stable memory as materials we use to record this age implode and crumble more rapidly than any papyrus or tablet? This led to meditations on film, on forms of propaganda, and the use of materials from newspapers.

The more I thought about this, the more I felt that it would somehow be disrespectful, certainly to the dead if not to the living, to pretend that I, as an individual, could add anything to all that has been said or written about war, genocide, exile, memory, and loss. I felt that, by adding new words, I would become a polluter and obfuscate the directions my other work had taken me in, particularly the translation. The issue was not to "say something" or impose an order upon the world but to recalibrate the relationship of existing materials to new conditions and interpretations dictated by events, current or otherwise. I had to let events read themselves back into the texts. I had to become my own translator and a translator of the cultural materials that had been given me or that I had gone in search of. It was with that realization that I decided to generate the texts from word lists and phrases derived from my reading. Through this process, for example, words generated from Shelley's "Revolt of Islam" could address the massacre at Srebrenica in our time. The process is really the opposite of a chance operation. By using the words of others, I was opening up a way of taking greater responsibility for them than if they were "mine." Inhabiting the world means there is no "other" not already in us, no capacities outside the human that can be attributed to anything outside what we ourselves are individually and collectively capable of.

Benjamin Hollander: Could you say something more about this idea of becoming your own translator? What do you mean by a process that is "the opposite" of a chance operation? Perhaps you could take me through the compositional process in your poetry...

Ammiel Alcalay: The processes of my own writing and translation effectively signal each other. I very much subscribe to the Jack Spicer mode of a radio receiver: if the frequencies are strong and I tune in, then the work is effortless, even though it might be exhausting. Having said that, I have gotten to a point of feeling at home with all the different kinds of things I do, so while all the rooms in the house (if you're lucky enough to have one) have a certain function, they are never exclusively that—in other words, you might read in the bathroom on occasion or eat in the bedroom. I find more and more that my work spills over from one designated area of activity to another. Teaching in a public place like Queens College—where it is common to have a class with twenty people speaking fifteen different languages—energizes and hones all these activities. When I give readings or lectures I've often pointed to a stack of my books on one side that includes scholarly works, political essays, and translations, and a very, very thin single volume of my poetic work on the other side, for example *the cairo notebooks*. I think that all the books in the big pile can be subsumed by the smaller volumes, which include this book, but I'm not so sure the reverse is true. Am I privileging the so-called creative or poetic aspects of my work? I don't think so. I think this has to do with a less easily defined quality. By saying that I've become a translator of my own work, I am struggling to define this quality. It has something to do with completeness on the one hand and with the inexhaustible on the other.

My book *After Jews & Arabs: Remaking Levantine Culture* was an attempt to employ a similar operation for the history of Jews and Arabs living and interacting over the past 1000 years—in a Levantine space. Initially, the Levant was a geographical term denoting the Eastern Mediterranean, but the term "Levantine" had taken on all kinds of pejorative qualities in the Israeli context, meaning impure, of undefined cultural background, mongrel, inferior, and so on. I finished the book in 1989 but it wasn't published until 1993. It has had a disproportional effect on all kinds of people and disciplines, perhaps because of its appeal across categories. I was amazed to recently discover that it was quoted at length by Prince Hassan of Jordan, at an interfaith conference held in Barcelona in 2000. It seems he turned to some of the Israeli delegates and said: "Is our region only about oil or weapons, is it not about human beings? From *After Jews & Arabs*, a book you probably know, by Professor Ammiel Alcalay, I quote…" That knocked me out—the Prince of Jordan quoting me to those who've made it a policy to ignore me! And he quoted the most poignant passage in the book, the end of the last paragraph: "Somewhere between visions based on the old prophesies, and the need for a new covenant, between the closed doors and the full streets, the magic of the old places and the locks of rooms without song, a space remains, a space for a poetics and a politics of the possible." Unfortunately, that hopeful vision of a space of possibility has been progressively undermined, often through brutal means.

The more I study and learn about the materials of the world, the more I am astonished at how I barely managed to scratch the surface, especially in that book. This is not true about poetic texts. When a poem tells you it's done, there is nothing more you can add or subtract. From there, it does its work. By contrast, knowledge is constantly shifting, there is always more one needs to know and add to the mix in order to further refine one's insights, rectify things that didn't pan out, or adjust for possibilities that get shut down. And events constantly inform history, retrospectively and prospectively. Knowledge must be applied in creating the poetic text, but the text—if it works—remains a step ahead, there is always more it can make room for. I find this when I re-read passages from *the cairo notebook*s in light of political contexts beyond the specifics of its own narrative. Here, I think, is the point of entry into processes of "translating myself" and making disparate materials speak to each other.

To refer, again, to *After Jews & Arabs*: it wasn't until three or four years after the book was published—following years of picking away at various aspects of Levantine culture, with its mix of languages, peoples, ideas, and forms—that I was even able to absorb what I had done. I needed other people to tell me that while I was defining this particular mélange of Islamic, Judeo-Arabic, Arabic, Sephardic, mizrahi, and Mediterranean Levantine culture, I had also redefined the whole idea of Europe! In other words, why wouldn't we begin to refer to figures like Maimonides, Ibn 'Arabi or Averroes as Europeans? After all, they were born in Europe, just as I was born in the United States.

The publishing history and controversies surrounding that book forced me to begin to look at intellectual disciplines in terms of labor relations. If a certain professor was considered an expert in European Studies, and was suddenly told that thinkers he or she had no knowledge of were foundations of this very culture, then such a person would have to be retrained. You can readily see the potential for anxiety here, particularly in the context of expertise on writing and the anti-intellectualism of many writing programs, especially given the role that "creative" writing is relegated to here.

When you translate, you become acutely aware of the engineering of texts, of how they are put together, of what's under the hood. Because of my practical bent and experiences in a variety of vocations—as auto mechanic, auto body worker, truck driver, carpenter, building super, laundromat manager, etc.—this appeals to me. The way I write poetry often involves a process of elimination. If a turn signal on a car doesn't work, you check the bulb and then the fuse. You might even find someone had tried fixing it before and there are wires leading nowhere. But you still trace all the wires back before you go tear the electrical system apart.

Let me give you an example: since the genocidal attack against Bosnia and the massacre at Srebrenica were central to *from the warring factions*, I immersed myself in all kinds of documents about them. I went through some 3,000 pages of UN documents, trying to pick out specific language that I might be able to use. All I ended up with were the few dry paragraphs towards the end of the third section of the poem, along with descriptions of uniforms worn by various militias, and a few odd words here and there. Most of it proved not very useful. Then, as I mentioned, I began generating word lists from Shelley's "Revolt of Islam." Now I had no particular reason to turn to that poem except one: it was one of the few texts by a canonical English writer in which the word Islam appears so prominently. It seemed to me that Shelley needed to meet these European Muslims whose remains were strewn across a small plot of land in Southern Europe, near a town that had once been a Roman silver mine. I made my choice not even particularly because of Shelley, though there are splendid passages on liberty and tyranny of his interspersed throughout that section, but because of those who would read Shelley, or anyone else for that matter, as if the materials were inert, inapplicable, academic.

Even though I was working with all of this, and much more, I don't think I was working any differently than I usually do. In some cases, a fragment from a letter, a particular line or phrase would become the kernel around which I would work the poems out. Particularly in the texts that are generated from word lists, I reached a point where I felt like a painter or a musician: *here are the materials I am able to work with.* Words became my scales or spectrum of colors and I could not go beyond them except through combination or juxtaposition. I found it enormously liberating. It eases the pressures, in many ways, of having to "say" something, and allows the language to dictate things back to you. By turning myself over to this process, it gives me greater freedom to deal with material that, if it were simply juxtaposed with "my own" writing, might be more likely to appear as, and be accused of, being mere appropriation. This charge, when dealing with such sensitive materials as quotations from survivors of genocide, must always be present—one has to seriously consider the consequences of appropriating such material. But if all the material is "appropriated," you create a different problematic.

As to this being the "opposite of a chance operation"… In a correspondence I had with our mutual friend the poet and translator Murat Nemet Nejat, Murat wrote me the following question: "I know of your admiration of Jackson Mac Low, though your technique may have nothing to do with his; I also know that Mac Low is not a 'mainstream' poet. Nevertheless, doesn't using a Western (though very experimental) technique become an obstacle to the audibility of the original voice? It will be easier for the Western reader to convert it into his or her frame of reference.

Shouldn't one find ways of "generating' from the original texts with methods more indigenous to the original literary and other traditions?" As you remember, we all met at the Kelly Writers House at the University of Pennsylvania. The title of our trialogue there was "Un-American Poetry," and we were each grappling with how our work is informed by "Un-American sources," even though we are all interested in and follow similar kinds of American poetry. My response to Murat was that I didn't see what I was doing as necessarily being a "Western" approach. Some of my earliest published poems are based on the old Roman *cento* form, in which there are no original lines. My own cues, I think, are taken much more from ancient Near Eastern and medieval Hebrew or Arabic practices where poems are interwoven with scriptural citations, often to startling effect. This is far from experimental and may even denote some kind of classical reserve. Medieval Hebrew poetry, for instance, which I have spent a lot of time studying, reading and translating, utilizes a practice called *shibbutz*—to embroider, inlay, ornament—which derives from the Arabic *al-iktibas*—"The lighting of a candle from a lamp already lit, or the kindling of a flame from a fire already blazing, perceived as an analogue to the Quran as source of light." Murat has developed similar ideas in relation to the grammatical structure of Turkish and the Turkish sufi tradition.

Wilson Harris's ideas about the need for "original epics" at a time of "cosmic abandonment" bear directly on this. He writes about a time when "the absolute commandment issued by a sovereign death-dealing regime is partial, and that partiality is threaded into inequalities, into injustices, harbored by one-sided traditions." Harris goes on: "Unless such absolutes can yield their partialities within plural masks that question themselves, the Soul is cut adrift and may lose its potency to arbitrate, with profoundest creativity, between divisions in humanity." This possibility of arbitration between divisions is essential for me, and the title of *from the warring factions* contains its ironies—there are political entities designated by others as "warring factions," but there are also warring factions within ourselves, within the structure of the family, within texts, within speech. I think here of Alice Notley reviving the epic, when she writes: "What a service to poetry it might be to steal story away from the novel & give it back to rhythm & sound." This is one of the reasons why I quote old prose of mine in the book, the furthest concession I'll make to novels in the conventional sense, in the context of a poem that is truly narrative. It's as if those short pieces—which stand out from the rest of the poem—encapsulate and suggest certain kinds of novels in and of themselves.

Benjamin Hollander: I am interested how you choose to imagine a situation differently in order to rethink politics. In your essay "Politics and Imagination," written days after the attacks on the Twin Towers in New York and published in Bosnia, you said that there was not only "a massive failure of intelligence gathering and security institutions" in the United States, but something "much deeper," "a failure" which was "conceptual and systemic," "permeating what Americans have allowed to enter their imaginative framework." You basically ask Americans to take an imaginative leap into a reality they refuse to see, a leap which might be in their interests if they could get *past* the politics of *self*-interest. For example, you say that "American intellectuals have never considered the fact that Arab intellectuals, almost by definition, are dissidents in very much the same way Eastern European intellectuals had been thought of during the Cold War," and that "Middle Eastern writers and thinkers who risk their lives find no resonance in the seat of imperial power, even among so many of those who would propose to be its conscience." Or, you say: "Americans, like anyone else, choose those aspects of the images they have of themselves to identify others, identify with others, or distance themselves from others. So Americans are channeled into identifying with the Israeli pioneer, like in the Wild West, and to distance themselves from Palestinians who, like Native Americans, were removed from their land… Palestinian and Arab literature is filled with imagery identifying the American Indian with the Palestinian."

Now we could probably quarrel about which Americans you mean (who they are and where they live, etc.), but it is your overall statement—concerning what Americans allow or don't allow into their "imaginative framework"—that makes me think more about how poetry might respond to the concerns you articulate in your essay, in particular, how *from the warring factions* tries to imagine a politics without becoming a conventionally "political" poem or a mere "sojourn." I'm not asking you to describe how you find analogs for "over there" in "the ground upon which one, or all of us, is standing," but how you think—if you do—that you have shaped the language of this book into a gesture which might re-imagine the politics of our lives and move us to interpret our world with more urgency—because we are startled into new or alternative visions by "the word."

Ammiel Alcalay: Let me come at this in a roundabout way. There is a pervasive monolingualism in American literary culture now, in the mainstream as well as in movements or groupings that might fit under some other rubric, whether "avant-garde," "oppositional," or otherwise. By "monolingualism," I mean the preponderance in the literate culture of no other immediate linguistic, cultural, or literary references outside American English. You can take this from television talk shows to tenure deliberations. I have seen university professors display difficulty understanding why a person coming up for tenure who is writing in their third or fourth language, and whose research requires at least five languages, should be thought of any differently than someone who has never read non-English sources on their subject, even if they exist and are significant. So I speak here not of writing per se, since I also write only in English, but of consciousness and awareness and involvement in other languages and cultural configurations. The language choice can be circumstantial or it can be crucial, but I still think that it is vitally important to give permission to other languages, literatures, and cultures to come into the space of the language you happen to be writing in. Monolingualism has not always been the case, and I think it is part of the Cold War legacy that is still very much with us. We are only at the very beginning of understanding the multilingual atmosphere in which writing and poetry in the United States has been produced, and continues to be produced. You yourself are an example, having heard and spoken, as you've told me, a limited, "broken" German and Hebrew before coming to the United States from Israel as a child, and how you've suggested this multilingual atmosphere might produce a "foreign" or alien poetry even within an English in which one appears "fluent."

In this regard, one can look at the remarkable work of Werner Sollors, for example, particularly his *Multilingual Anthology of American Literature* (with Marc Shell), which introduces texts from Massachussett, Italian, Arabic, Lenape, French, Spanish, German, Polish, Russian, Welsh, Yiddish, Swedish, Norwegian, Navajo, Hebrew, Danish, Chinese, Greek, and other languages. For Sollors, these are all constituents of American literature. There are plenty of examples like this, even in canonized modernists. Gertrude Stein, Louis Zukofsky, or William Carlos Willams—all spoke other languages as children, as did Jack Kerouac, someone one doesn't normally think of in this context. Not to mention the enormous presence of Spanish, the whole

Nuyorican movement, different Chicano writers, Native American writers exposed to people retaining their own languages, Italian American writers who grew up with Italian, Asian American writers who grew up with other languages, more and more South Asian writers coming out of Urdu and Bengali, Arab American writers coming out of Arabic, and so on.

The problem is that there is no lasting recognition; these things get viewed as curiosities, rather than as fundamental. A certain model has been set up, almost of sampling or dabbling, in which at this point we are presented more often than not with translations made by people who don't even know the languages they are translating from, much less the social and historical contexts they purport to be transmitting. Yet these things are still called translations. Such productions take up cultural space and make it that much more difficult to transmit the real, in this case some sense and context of where a text might be placed socially and historically in the culture it comes from. In effect, such productions produce ignorance. We are collectively impoverished by this, and more than handicapped. There is very little institutionalization, in the good sense, of the need to know languages, to immerse oneself in other cultures. One indication of this, for me, is that while there are many writers coming out of different linguistic backgrounds, very few have chosen to re-immerse themselves in their language or culture and translate.

Benjamin Hollander: You're right in a way, but I also don't think doing translation, in and of itself, would be a litmus test for writers of different linguistic backgrounds to measure the sincerity or urgency of their immersion in a multilingual consciousness. In fact, and not so ironically, we know of writers whose parochialism can be seen precisely *through* their translations, while there are others who have never translated yet whose work in various ways is informed by a multilingual consciousness.

Ammiel Alcalay: Absolutely! Your work, or the work of Myung Mi Kim—actually, I can think of many, like Sesshu Foster, Kamau Braithwaite, Victor Hernandez Cruz, and others I've mentioned like Shihab Nye and Herrera, or Majid Naficy, whose mesmerizing *Muddy Shoes* is in some sense the obverse, translated from the Persian but taking place in an American context and consciousness—there are numerous examples of how one can be informed by a multilingual consciousness without being involved in the specific kind of translation or transmission I do. At the same time, there are some who translate who don't necessarily contribute to any exploratory or displacing movement in American English—they can even work counterproductively, setting limitations, making things definitive where they should be expansive, orderly where they should be disruptive, exclusive where they should be inclusive. We're talking about symptoms of a larger issue, a kind of collective intellectual failure—a general submission to the dominance of monolingualism as I've defined it.

For a writer not to know and read and engage several other languages seems to me to be like a musician playing only one note, or a painter who has decided to just use blue crayons. I read Hebrew, what used to be called Serbo-Croatian, French, Spanish, and Italian and I struggle with Latin and Arabic, but I still don't think it's either particularly remarkable or nearly enough, given how common this is for many in the rest of the world. Most of all, a monolingual consciousness allows cultural and governmental commissars to assume and promote limited perspectives and be secure in knowing that there is little basis for deeply rooted social or cultural resistance, especially to lies and stereotypes. This is internalized; it is also reproduced socially across the body politic, from the campaign against terrorism, to a special on foreign presses I recently saw in the magazine *Poets & Writers* in which the section on Israel featured only white Ashkenazis. The same journalists and editors would have been outraged to see a feature on New York or Los Angeles that did not mention African Americans, Asians, or Latinos. But in Israel they didn't know what to look for or, more importantly, didn't know what they weren't being shown. While so many students are out there doing hyper-theoretical work on a limited number of texts, we still don't have a map. People need to go back and do a kind of socio-linguistic and cultural atlas of what has taken place and continues to take place in this country. It would be revealing and might dislodge assumptions about who and what we are or claim to be. It would also make it easier to see things.

In 1999, I explored how Edward Said dealt with this in his memoir: "In many ways, the memoir itself seems a long-delayed reaction against some of [Said's] earliest and most acute impressions of American behavior, as when he writes of 'the extraordinary homogenizing power of American life,' which 'seemed to limit the complex discourse of daily life to an unreflective minimum in which memory has no role.' Part of this need to reassert and validate personal experience also comes as an antidote to the very marked American tendency to relegate individuals to the role of surrogates, standing in as representatives of the race, the tribe or anything not completely domesticated or reducible to the already known. The most immediate form of this, of course, occurs through naming and the pronunciation of 'non-American' names. The accessibility of being named Edward proved deceptive to Said, and the ways in which realities left behind were either mispronounced or left unpronounced is clearly another major theme of his memoir. As an extension of this practice of domesticating things whose names we cannot utter, Said's role and persona is often referred to, tongue in cheek, using classically anti-Semitic terminology—as someone so much like the 'rootless, cosmopolitan Jewish intellectual.' That is, someone almost like us but whom we can still hold at arm's length by not fully embracing their own context, by distancing them again, using terms familiar to us."

Said describes an "unreflective minimum in which memory has no role." This is clearly connected to the ideology of capitalism and consumption, with its technological imperative to constantly produce new models, whether of automobiles or poems. This is one of the reasons why I became so interested in translating texts that appear formally conventional to people brought up, let's say, on the pyrotechnics of work under the designated rubric of postmodernism or what has come to be called Language Poetry. It is exceedingly difficult for such readers to recalibrate themselves to the nuances of texts whose innovations are not technical. These nontechnical nuances appear either as incremental or radical changes in consciousness; through their depiction of a coming to awareness, they disclose the reproduction of a social order and the writer's intervention in it.

Here, perhaps, I would take slight issue with your designation of the conventionally "political" poem, and refer to a book of essays, *Line Break: Poetry as Social Practice* by James Scully, that remains completely relevant. He speaks, for example, of the American chapter of P.E.N. and its "Freedom to Write Committee," something that, for all intents and purposes, appears "progressive." Scully writes: "In the U.S., where nearly a third of the population is functionally illiterate, that organization has not made literacy a priority. Yet the freedom to be literate, especially as no one is naturally illiterate, would seem, in the absence of class bias, cause for overriding concern."

In relation to what I just spoke about—texts that appear conventional but depict a coming-to-consciousness—Scully speaks about a 19th-century trend, *Tendenz*, associated with the Young Germany Movement, and also called "committed writing" or "tendency" poetry. Scully writes: "Here is a poetry conscious of living social context: what it is becoming and what it is coming up against. In idealist poetries the awareness of limits induces fatalism, cynicism, sentimentality. It reinforces the stupefying belief that truth is relative, that the fragments of experience cannot be added up—as they cannot be if experience is conceived subjectively, in isolation, rather than socially. But in tendency poetry the encounter with limits is an encounter. It produces historical specificity. The fact is that truth isn't relative, it's historical. This isn't something that can be learned. We have to keep on learning it. It is arrived at through personal social struggle. There are no shortcuts."

In a curious sense, by giving up my own limitations as a "creator" and turning to the words of others to compose my poem, I am re-enacting the limitlessness of this historical specificity. To the uninitiated, this may seem like an abyss, but I would say instead that whatever produces such "fatalism, cynicism and sentimentality" is far more abysmal.

An example of this lack of preparedness that I spoke of earlier, and not only amongst writers and intellectuals in the US following September 11th, can be seen in the kinds of poems people chose to circulate after that event, as if they could at all sum up or even relate to the experience we had just witnessed. One by Auden particularly unnerved me, and seemed more like a sympathy card. It wasn't so much the poem ("9/1/39"), but the use made of it. One can compare, as I've done elsewhere, the writing and exile of Joseph Brodsky (who wrote on this poem) with the writing and exile of Darwish or Laabi. The difference, it seems to me, has to do with the idea that there might be such a thing as a pure, objectified art which is then opposed to "engaged" or "committed" writing, rather than pursuing writing which is always simply part of a more general social and political condition. This comes back to the distinctions I made earlier between formally "sophisticated" and "naive" work. In other words, in these literate circles, even after such an event, we got exactly what could be expected—no one had the wherewithal to think of circulating poetry that might have something to say to the matters at hand, that might have reverberated with the worlds these attacks demanded we pay attention to—something by Darwish, for instance, or the Iraqi poet Saadi Yusef. The Auden poem operated as a cipher, standing in for a lack of connection to something that would require more serious striving to get at.

Benjamin Hollander: It's interesting to contrast the use of Auden's poem as a "cipher" to limit an historical moment of crisis, even as those who quote it would claim to make it ideally stand in for that moment, and your notion of limiting yourself as a creator and "turning to the words of others to compose [your] poem" to "re-enact the limitlessness of this historical specificity." The first seems to me to reflect what Paul Goodman called "The Psychology of Being Powerless." Since we are historically unprepared for the crisis, since we don't know where to look for the references which would immediately speak to us, we either withdraw from, or "rationally" identify with, the very systems of power which generated the crisis. I suppose one way for unprepared writers and intellectuals to do this is to look back in time, choose a poem that will speak for us, and appear rational and "sensitive" in playing the sympathy card. This nostalgic act assumes some kind of delusional command over the moment. It keeps the crisis in a "chronic low-grade emergency" (Goodman) and says "we've got it under control" when we don't, because, as you said earlier, we are really without context, not knowing what to look for or, more importantly, not knowing "what [we aren't] being shown." Your practice of citings, by contrast, encourages us to return to where we stand or where we might soon stand.

To say: look here, under here, over here. They are historical jump cuts, but they are aligned; they name, they accuse. In that sense, one question you're addressing is how poetry as a return to knowledge can heighten our consciousness of the critical emergencies of this moment, and future moments, by transforming our imagination of history. These voices in poetry speak as witnesses among witnesses from the warring factions: it's a way of giving us a map and redrawing it at the same time. The other day a student from Ramallah with very little English asked to add one of my critical thinking / writing classes. I asked what he was studying. He said Engineering. I asked if he was interested in poetry. He said no. "So you don't know the poetry of Mahmoud Darwish or Samih al-Qasim?" I asked. He jumped on me: "Why of course!" he said, looking puzzled. Another student in an introductory poetry class once innocently asked me why Charles Reznikoff's long poem "Holocaust" wasn't taught in History. "Yes," I said, "why not?" So it seems to me that the way you're writing into language and history has larger implications beyond this book, in that it questions the boundaries we've drawn around what we let in or exclude from our understanding of poetic practice, and from how we think and act in relation to the world in a time of emergency. Would it be accurate, for example, to say that as you're sourcing history in poetry, you're questioning poetry's role in our (American) culture, and asking: how is it read and how can it be read, by whom and for whom, and how can we see writing as "always part of a more general social and political condition"?

Ammiel Alcalay: When you mention "poetry as a return to knowledge," "transforming our imagination of history," these are huge ideas that poets seem to studiously avoid or are just not sure how to deal with, given the climate we are working in. In a review of Charles Olson's letters, I spoke of him as a "public intelligence" rather than what we now so uncritically call a "public intellectual." While Olson has been villified for a variety of things, the political foundation of his work, as Amiri Baraka has pointed out, has been completely elided, almost disappeared. The turning away from a grounded poetics and the backlash against its concerns in much of what is now in vogue seem to me a great loss of breadth and scope, a willingness to not only settle for less but to become domesticated and so willingly participate in, and accept, structures of power. This relates to your earlier question about urgency and new or alternative visions that may or may not be represented in the book. Here I would expand on something I spoke of earlier, about labor relations in the intellectual realm. I think that the way I work, both in the books and across the roles and activities that I've taken on, has—or should indeed have —wider implications. While my discursive work more obviously points to boundaries that need to be reconsidered, redrawn, or abolished, I think that *from the warring factions* questions things that have now become part of poetic practice, decorum or, to be more blunt, the job market. We have pretty much come to the point of removing poetry from knowledge, and sticking it in the creative department, which then is taken to be something like what the "Negro Leagues" once represented. While many of our most suggestive and fertile theoretical models have been written by poets, space for public intellectual life—or public intelligence—is almost non-existent outside the academy, and even inside it. Given the status of poets as "natives"—those unworthy of speaking for themselves outside the boundaries of a "creative" reserve within this academic / intellectual configuration—these models usually end up ignored or bypassed.

We all know some of the classic texts in this vein, the writing of Gertrude Stein, *Call Me Ishmael* by Charles Olson, *Bottom: On Shakespeare* by Louis Zukofsky, *My Emily Dickinson* by Susan Howe, *Genoa* by Paul Metcalf, *Blues*

People by Amiri Baraka—all are examples that come to mind. Such texts are still being produced—I would say that David Meltzer's set *Writing Jazz* and *Reading Jazz* should be at the forefront of theoretical and practical studies in a variety of fields. But this is even less likely to happen now that segments of "oppositional" poetic movements have become thoroughly institutionalized. Within academic culture, English departments have been able to fence writers off in the fiercely anti-intellectual "safe-havens" of MFA programs, setting the parameters and controlling the critical / theoretical discourse about writing. Poets, typically, remain beyond the pale and, like many "minorities," too often concede to the anti-intellectual stereotypes applied to them.

My experiences in Israel, as I've said earlier, were instructive in this regard. The mainstream literary critic and arbiter of taste Gershon Shaked decided, at some point a number of years ago, to include several non-mainstream writers in a history of contemporary Hebrew literature. Two of these novelists, Shimon Ballas and Sami Michael, are both from Baghdad and were involved in Leftist politics. Shaked said their political attitudes were formed as an angry reaction to how they were treated as Iraqi Jews in Israeli society. In an article called "Rehabilitation or Libel?" Ballas denounced Shaked as a racist, writing that if an Ashkenazi had political attitudes, it would be the result of free choice, personal preference, intellectual tendency, or some other willed attitude. But for Ballas and Michael, such attitudes could not be self-willed, they had to be a reaction against something done to them, removing any form of autonomous power or will. This, I think, does indeed reveal the essence of racism. It is worthwhile considering how similar attitudes or categorizations constrain us all.

Juan Goytisolo, in his essay "On Literature Considered as a Criminal Activity," speaks about the role of writers in freer and less free societies. In permissive or liberal societies, "provocation" must be interiorized, "introduced into language itself." But this provocation, as we know all too well, can be co-opted: "We arrive here at the very root of the problem. Is it possible for the writer, for the intellectual, to preserve their potential criminality from the dangers that the ever-enjoyable and desirable regime of permissiveness brings with it? Does the disappearance of the risk of punishment, whether physical (prison, banishment, internment in an asylum) or exclusively material or moral (forbidding the right to work, loss of a job, ostracism) automatically presuppose the end of ethical yet socially transgressive behavior, of literature as an occupation made synonymous with the criminal act by a silent and morally upright majority?" These questions are always with me, particularly since I know and have been involved with so many writers and friends in various parts of the world whose freedoms are not guaranteed and whose sense of urgency is heightened because of wars, military occupations, or repressive circumstances. This exerts a sense of positive pressure on the freedom I have, and makes me want to stretch it to the limits practically and politically. When I first corresponded with Abraham Serfaty, a political prisoner in Morocco for over twenty years, he was still in jail and he wrote me how helpful it had been for him to follow the work that I was doing on mizrahi culture and politics. When my friend the Lebanese novelist Elias Khoury organized a commemoration of the 50th year of the Palestinian Nakba (disaster), in Beirut in 1998, and took great risks by dedicating several days to an examination of the fate of Arab Jews, I responded with something to stretch analagous borders constraining the discourse I am involved in here. In that sense, my poetic work is very personal in an altogether different way than we usually define it.

The politics I want to re-enact in *from the warring factions* have to do with bringing knowledge and history back in at the point where they have become almost non-existent in our poetic culture, and to do it in a form that questions various conventions and fixed ideas, whether mainstream or "avant-garde." To do this is like bringing up things in polite conversation that people would rather not talk about. In using Hannah Arendt's phrase "borrowed time" for the title of the fourth section of the poem, and juxtaposing it with a poem composed with words from the enslaved African-American poet Phillis Wheatley, I wanted to re-enact, and address, a deep rift in the United States, one I am surely part of, that is the conflict between voluntary immigration and enslavement. The consequences of this rift are perpetually reproduced socially. These kinds of things remain abstract for people whose social and cultural contacts are circum-scribed in a homogeneous class or language.

When I think about the kinds of people whose work matters to me, and the risks so many of them have taken in adverse situations, it makes me very aware, as a writer, of who it is I actually want to address. Given the state the world is in, blissful ignorance is beneath contempt. Polite discourse of any kind merely feeds the war machinery. By making words and languages reorient themselves across time and face each other under new conditions, my inten-tion is to re-awaken the ancient force of poetry—as fact and testimony.

—Conducted 2001-2002

a note on
materials & processes

The first section of *from the warring factions*, "Old Bridge," consists of my words, except for the Adolph Gottlieb quote and the line from Barry McGuire's "Eve of Destruction." There are quotes from *the cairo notebooks*, and a number of sections in the book where I make use of words generated from writing of mine dating back, in some cases, to the 1970s.

The second section, "no place / not rome," for the poet Jerry Estrin, began as a dedication to his life and a meditation on his remarkable poem on the Gulf War, "Rome, A Mobile Home." This was the most explicit poetic reference I had encountered that spoke directly to the idea of American empire in that war, relating it to Rome. There is a prefiguration here of what is named "migration / hegira" in the next section. Virgil, sometimes thought of as the quintessential imperial poet, is here used as an emblem of one who knows what price one must pay for power, and that it must result in the death of loved ones, in the *Aeneid* both the hero Aeneas's friend and companion Palinurus, and his lover Dido.

If my poem is an epic, and it has a hero, then that hero is William Haglund, mentioned right at the beginning of "no place / not rome," and at key intervals later in the poem. Haglund is a forensic anthropologist whose mother had been stabbed to death by an estranged lover. In the mid-1960s he got a degree in mortuary science and became an embalmer in, of all places, Whittier, California. In the 1980s, he worked as a forensic investigator in Seattle where he was involved in the investigation of the Green River killings. By the mid 1980s, Haglund was involved in training students to identify the bodies of the disappeared in Argentina. He moved on to train people in Chile and Guatemala. In the 1990s, Haglund worked in the former Yugoslavia as well as Rwanda. Information on all this can be found in *The Graves: Srebrenica and Vukovar*, by Eric Stover and Gilles Peress.

There are very few pieces in "no place / not rome" using

my words; most are generated from a variety of texts that include my correspondence with Jerry Estrin, the letters of Sacco and Vanzetti, Jane Harrison, Carl Sauer, Thomas Nashe, Hannah Arendt, political speeches and phrases from the Gulf War (Dick Cheney, George Bush Sr., Marlin Fitzwater, et. al.), Tacitus, Plutarch, Lucan's *Pharsalia*, Virgil, Hippocrates, Empedocles, Herodotus, the *Quran*, pre-Islamic poetry, the *Zohar*, Ibn 'Arabi, Chaucer, Dryden, Emerson, Melville's *Clarel*, Robert Duncan, Duncan McNaughton, Lisa Robertson, Leonard Cohen, Hank Williams, gossip magazines on Liz Taylor as Cleopatra, the film scripts of *The Last of the Mohicans* and *Rebel Without a Cause*, and Danny Lyon's *The Destruction of Lower Manhattan*, a work that, ironically enough, records the obliteration of the leather, butter, and milk districts to make room for the building of the World Trade Center.

The third section of the book, "migration / hegira," spreads in both space and time, undergirding everything with Native American and Ancient Near Eastern material. The allusion to Native America is set from the first section, with the arrowhead found by my neighbor in his backyard in Brooklyn. The magnet drawing everything towards it in this section is the 1995 massacre at Srebrenica. Here I relied on a documentary film by Leslie Woodhead, *Srebrenica: A Cry from the Grave* (BBC2 / PBS, 1999), particularly quotations from Bosnian survivors Hasan Nuhanović, Saliha Osmanović and Zumra Sheikhomerović, all of whom lost parents, husbands, or sons. There are also quotations from Jean Renè Ruiz, a criminal investigator from France who worked for the War Crimes Tribunal, UN documents, including *Annexes of the Final Report of UN Commission of Experts on War Crimes in the Former Yugoslavia*, documents from the International War Crimes Tribunal in the Hague, and quotations from General Ratko Mladić, Cyrus Vance, Yasushi Akashi, and Thorwald Stoltenberg. Other materials in this section include the *Book of Kings, Ezekiel*, Shelley's "Revolt of Islam" and other texts, Walt Whitman, Robert Frank, *Letters from Nantucket and Martha's Vineyard* by J. Hector St. John de Crèvecoeur, Jack Spicer, the *Walam Olam* (translated by Joe Napora), Louis Zukofsky, George Oppen, Black Elk, communiqués of Egyptian student demonstrations from 1946 as recorded by the historian Ahmed Abdalla, quotations from Israeli human rights lawyer Lea Tsemel, *A Survey of Palestine* (prepared in December 1945 and January 1946 for the Anglo-American Committee of Inquiry), Germaine Tillion, Mouloud Feraoun, *Orientalism and Architecture* by Owen Jones, Christopher Marlowe, Emily Dickinson, a forgotten but great American novelist by the name of George Mandel, James M. Cain, Cornell Woolrich, and Carson McCullers, among others. In some cases, I needed to go after specific material, in other cases I looked for language that might fit a certain mood. Since Srebrenica was a crime, I looked for language in Woolrich and Cain.

The title of the fourth section—the Hannah Arendt phrase where she says that we are all now living on "borrowed time"—comes from her *On Revolution*. The words in this section are American, even though some, such as Arendt's and those of Phillis Wheatley and others, come from people transported to these shores, voluntarily or in chains. In this section, the dispossession of those who have gone to war comes out clearly, alluded to earlier in the text with the Roman sources, now through the stories of veterans, particularly the Navajo code talkers who waited so long for the state to recognize what they had done. Material here includes words from John Wieners, *The Book of Daniel Drew*, the Pequot convert William Apess, Langston Hughes, Ralph Ellison, James Baldwin, Duke Ellington, Sidney Bechet, Yusef Lateef, Sun Ra, Melvin Tolson, the 1847 *Narrative of William Wells Brown, A Fugitive Slave*, the African-American whaling captain William A. Martin, Tecumseh, William Henry Harrison, and the artist Jess.

The title of the last section, "night of unity," refers to an Egyptian Jewish ceremony dating from the 12th century and probably based on Sufi practice. The ceremony takes place at the first full moon before Passover and recounts the parting of the Red Sea, in an Arabic text that is both celebratory and solemn. The section begins with some lines from a testimony that I took from Faisal Husseini, the late Palestinian leader, describing a man he met in prison telling of the sinking of a boat heading to Lebanon during the Camps War in the 1980s. This returns me to the atmosphere and conditions of *the cairo notebooks*. This whole section is a political and literary commentary on all that has preceded it; it is also the only section dominated by quoting whole blocks of text. Crucial sources here include the great historian Hanna Batatu's *The Old Social Classes and the Revolutionary Movement in Iraq: A Study of Iraq's Old Landed Commercial Classes and its Communists, Ba'athists and Free Officers*, descriptions of sections of Saddam Hussein's novel *Zabiba and the King*, excerpts of letters from (my interviewer) Benjamin Hollander, a letter from Duncan McNaughton, descriptions of the CIA's overthrow of Mossadegh in Iran in 1953, quotations from *Everything and Nothing* (2000), a video by Jayce Salloum about the Lebanese prisoner Soha Bishara, held in Khiam detention center for ten years, more references to the forensic anthropologist William Haglund, and the early writings on film by the poet Vachel Lindsay.

Other texts provided important material from which word lists were generated: *The Graves: Srebrenica and Vukovar*, by Eric Stover and Gilles Peress, *Early Islamic Mysticism*, translated by Michael Sells, *Writing Jazz* by David Meltzer, *Image of the New World* by Gordon Brotherston and Ed Dorn, *Skull Wars* by David Hurst Thomas, *The Name of War* by Jill Lepore, *The Invasion of America* by Francis Jennings, *Indian New England Before the Mayflower* by Howard S. Russell, *Native Peoples of Southern New England, 1500-1650* by Kathleen Bragdon, *Native Names of New England Towns and Village*s by C. Laurence Bond, *Pontiac and the Indian Uprising* by Howard H. Peckham, *Our Hearts Fell to the Ground*, edited by Collin Calloway, *The Language of America* by Roger Williams, *American Indian Prose and Poetry* by Margot Astrov, and our paper of record, *The New York Times.*

further notes,
addenda, & bios

AUTHOR'S NOTE TO THE NEW EDITION

from the warring factions begins December 1st, 1993 and ends August 2nd, 2001. Preceded by the Gulf War, the decimating sanctions on Iraq and the wars of ex-Yugoslavia, and followed by 9/11 and the second assault against Iraq, the book took up a huge block of time, even though most of the final writing was done quickly in early summer of 2001. Ten years have passed since the first publication of the book in 2002, and I can now see more clearly how the form the material demanded created ripple effects that have extended forward and backward.

Aware that *from the warring factions* fell outside the conceptual purview of almost any publisher I could think of, I was perplexed where to turn when I had finished it. That began what has been a more than ten-year working dialogue with writer, editor, and publisher Fred Dewey. The crucial elements of his approach are conceptual, placing facets together to set a book's after-life into motion. The importance of the book as physical object is enhanced by its moving parts, from the relationship of the cover image to the image on the inside cover, from the body of the text to its accompanying materials—and here, for the new edition, with the inclusion of an introduction by Diane di Prima. Conceptualizing the book in this way forces the author to become a reader. In my case, the after-effects forced me to consider the biography that had been presented in my conversation with Benjamin Hollander—a unit of the book proposed and thought out to complement the poem—in light of my use of sources in the poem itself. From this remove, I think it is important to let the conversation stand as a record, despite whatever changes my thinking has gone through since, misgivings I might have about the stridency of some of that thought, or the pressure to create a kind of display or update the overall record.

There are points at which the conversation now seems far too one-sided, and it would have benefited from a less catalogic and more dialogic approach. What remains crucial, though, is how this awareness was propelled by the book itself. By framing the object as a spur to new activity, the book provided a vehicle through which I could revisit versions of how I had cast the relative significance of my own experience at different times.

As the book came together, I witnessed and participated in a breakdown of journalistic / critical print culture and the venues and modes of address associated with its production. We haven't even begun to address the paralytic cultural and political effects of this breakdown in the United States or the intellectual and emotional vacuum left in its wake. It is as if phantom limbs have been strewn every which way with no map or guide to chart to whom they once belonged. Nothing has come to replace the complex, material nexus of relations that were the basis of the immediacy of human and vocational interaction, from paper-making and printing to trucks and delivery, from design and shipping to the space of encounter at a newsstand.

This was already starting to become evident to me several weeks after I had finished the book, through an interview I did with Emir Imamović and Ivan Lovrenović for the Bosnian weekly *DANI*, "After the Fall of Communism, the West Finds its Enemy in Islam," and published in Sarajevo just a few days prior to 9/11. Such discussion had already become impossible to conduct in the United States. Now, a decade later, those magazines—so courageous and full of true critical thinking during and for some years after the war—no longer exist, dissolved by media conglomeration brought on by IMF structural adjustment, accommodation to the apartheid solution of the Dayton Accords, and aspirations to enter the European Union. The Bosnian institutions that managed to survive the war have fallen victim to assassination by administrative fiat. The Dayton Accords, which gave equal power to the perpetrators of the genocidal attack on Bosnia-Hercegovina, have it in their means to cut funding and accomplish economically what was impossible to do militarily. As of the start of 2012, seven institutions—including the 125-year-old National Museum housing the six-hundred-year-old manuscript known as the Sarajevo Haggadah, and the National Library—have shut their doors. Western diplomacy has achieved what massacres, mass rape, concentration camps, deportation, and dynamite were unable to: the destruction of Bosnia's shared cultural heritage. And so the post-war survivors find themselves fighting an enemy woven into the very fabric of the social and ideological structure. The significance of this for civic life everywhere —for repositories of public memory such as libraries, for models of coercive ethnic and religious division in so-called strategic regions and in American domestic policy—remains all but ignored. As poet Marko Vešović writes: "My God, the speechlessness / all around me, harder to pierce than tank armor."

At this remove, I can say that *from the warring factions*, in addition to its obvious form as a poem, is journalism and scholarship by other means. Like many before me, "tempting" different kinds of expression, a poem seemed the only vessel that could take on everything I was grappling with: raw data, historical and political artifacts, the record of fractured chronologies, wildly disparate registers of language and emotion, and the simple fact of singular instances of expression only fully embodied in sound and syntax. As Muriel Rukeyser so clearly put it, "the poem can extend the document." And the application of Charles Olson's methodology by Ed Sanders, in his formulation of "investigative poetics," marks the imperative: "that poetry should again assume the responsibility for the description of history." This, in turn, has been taken up by Kristin

Prevallet, when she writes: "Through these practices, poetry is infused with the flow of larger reality, a space occupied with objects in constant motion, and with people—us— who exist in relation to both our personal histories, our political inheritance, and the strata of the land upon which we're standing."

While I've often thought it necessary to explore lengthy bibliographies of useful references that might create the context for a poem I am reading, I worked in reverse here, seeking ways to condense enormous amounts of research into the poem I was writing. I was able to boil down large swaths of material I had encountered over years into abbreviated versions that—contextualized by and in the poem— could be more immediately effective and understandable. The use of very select quotes, for example, from Hana Batatu's inordinately dense 1,280-page masterpiece *The Old Social Classes and the Revolutionary Movements in Iraq: A Study of Iraq's Old Landed and Commercial Classes and of its Communists, Ba'thists, and Free Officers*, at least posited the reality of that prodigious work as a resource for understanding Sadaam Hussein's Iraq and the times we were living through. And once put in the poem, like Shelley's words taken from "The Revolt of Islam" (used in the last four poems in the third section), a whole further set of imaginings, growing out of these juxtapositions, becomes available. Embedding my own history and older writing in the poem demanded it be further explored, and the after-effects set in motion by the construction of the book instigated other books. But it also led me to reread my own work, and realize that my uses of citation dated back much earlier, to the mid-1970s, evolving through my 1993 *cairo notebooks*, to even more urgently face the crisis of testimony, appropriation, and the use of sources in *from the warring factions.*

While Olson had already defined the problem back in the late 1940s as one of inundation, of over-information, and the need to cut the knot—to use the critical function in the collection of the materials in order to make fact fable again—certain forms over the past decade have seemed to embrace information only to get lost in it. I was aware of this, inundated as I was by information during years of gathering material for this book, and knowing that a unique form needed to be found to get such materials back into circulation. One prevalent approach (what has fashionably developed into so-called "conceptual poetry") downplays or disappears the kind of concrete engagement with materials and form taken up in *factions*, in which the weight of words—on a cellular and historical level—are propelled back into circulation precisely to collide with memory and event, where the "personal" is of necessity both public and political. This engagement can accept neither a flattened-out, digitized-and-pixilated version of the world nor the purported political efficacy of re-circulating only words hatched under viral conditions. This "conceptual" as it now stands seems to work more like a holding pen, a place of quarantine, in which contamination is held in check or circulates in a closed loop. And it occupies space, displacing not only critical thought but that poetry which, as Prevallet has noted, enacts "the work of radical linguistic, contextual, and metrical articulation."

The use of an investigative method and a conceptual framework to generate poetic work engaging political situations, and the language emerging from those situations, has been picked up in the intervening years. Looking at such work has allowed me, as a reader, to reconsider what I was trying to do in *factions*, clarifying why it might have resonated among those looking for new approaches to charged material. Writers can assume authority over a subject without revealing how they might have arrived at such authority. In the end, however, application of method to an ostensible subject must be differentiated from tracking a historicized self and the enactment of revealing consciousness through the process and progress of the work itself. This, of course, brings us back to Olson's "fable," to the story, to narrative, to the idea of changing selves over time in the midden of historical contingency.

At a reading in Vancouver in 2010, I talked through some of these ideas about narrative, what the probing of evidence about one's past selves might yield, and used the figure of memory ballasts, anchors to a more distant past that I had dropped at various places in my work and had been going back not necessarily to retrieve but see why I had left there in the first place. I was struck by a response from poet and novelist Daphne Marlatt: "There seems to be a lot of motion, a lot of movement, you're using long sentences, that's what it sounds like, it's what gets caught up in a sentence that generates the narrative." Beyond the expected imperatives —that political life is inextricably bound to possibilities of expression, to what gets called so generally "culture," removed from worship, rites, or tillage—what remains is an ongoing struggle with form, with what something turns out to be and how it gets to be that way. To move from the obviously historical to the less obviously historical, to situate ourselves in time and understand how we got here, to find what is ours in order to disown it—that movement is the story, and an essential part of the task that *from the warring factions* sought, and seeks again, to engage.

—Ammiel Alcalay
July, 2012

ADDENDA FROM THE EDITOR

Ammiel Alcalay and I met in Los Angeles in the late 1990s when he came to read at Beyond Baroque, a literary center I ran in Los Angeles (and would continue to run until 2010). I edited and published books at the Center using materials and images to form a "site" for the works, a kind of public space expressed visually, textually, and objectively. My intention was to engender further work, concept, and dialogue, on the page and in the world. Eager to publish Alcalay's book-length poem, back then before 9/11, I began to discuss ideas about format with him, moving quickly to broader issues of poetics, culture, and politics. A strong, mutual dissatisfaction with how things were being done set principles into motion: out of this came *from the warring factions* (with its images and set of materials), Benjamin Hollander's *Vigilance*, anthologies, the *OlsonNow* series, and some of the original concepts propelling Alcalay's *Lost & Found* series at CUNY in New York. Most of all, our conversations led to a rethinking of our own histories as a way to grapple with the stakes of culture and poetics. Alcalay's enormously influential lectures on Charles Olson—forming part of a second book of his I have edited for re: public, *a little history*—began in this work and the concerns that were launched here.

As Alcalay suggests, facts can find a proper home if we make the effort to give them one. But facts are under siege. We face what one might call *defactualization*—the constant, deliberate, organized undoing of facts and factuality by the political order and its society. In regarding responses to this, one thinks immediately of Hannah Arendt's attempt, after WWII, to return lost, stolen, or abandoned objects to their proper owners. This is, in a certain way, what culture is, and it constitutes a fight and struggle, possibly the most crucial one. Objects and people do not just need to belong, they *belonged*. This past matters because it forms our present, and without it, our present floats in a dangerous state. We remain connected to place, to land, to things and people, yet face dispossession, dislocation, and worse, as if without recourse.

Returning Alcalay's poem to print, after many trials, is possible because of those who have generously helped. Notable among them are the editors at UpSet Press who believed in the creation of a new edition for this book, helping to get it out to new readers. While the object now constitutes a new "site," its core carries forward from the past. The long poem forming the heart of the book and the conversation with Benjamin Hollander are unaltered, save for minor corrections. Alcalay laments in his new note that this conversation at the back is one-sided (it is a kind of multiple launching point for trips out and back). I pushed for this new note and to expand the conversation then, and am responsible for their inclusion, having requested the author dig deeper into his working principles. Adding Diane di Prima's introduction helps pinpoint the stakes and bring out the poem's *gestus*—to use Brecht's useful term for the way a work can, and will, act into the world. One is grateful to have di Prima to point us in—as she has in the past so often, and will continue to for all of us. She is a challenger and this text deserves to be introduced by a partisan for the world.

In a time when warring factions are used, deployed, and triggered, civil war exported as a manufacture, it seems fitting an inhabitant of its leading artificer engage one case of this in poetic terms, to discover how poetics might finally take up the burden of our times and respond. The response to conditions and materials is what Alcalay's book is all about, and it is quite experimental and bold for that. Regardless of what theories one has as to why the specific massacres in Srebrenica happened, the poem is dedicated to the city. And therein lies the story. People, places, and things recover a chance to speak and be heard, to see and be seen, to face and be faced—that is, to *respond*, to *occasion* response, in the actual world. The poem shapes a kind of *polis* of resonant things and people, and, as it were, answers Juan Goytisolo's later, April, 2006 answer to the probings of *The New York Times*: "I am the son not of my mother, but of the civil war, its messianism, its hatred." This disavowal points to our responsibilities, our dislocations, and even our genesis. Alcalay makes this concrete and spatial.

Stories and meanings and memories are progeny too. They have a relation to contingency and specificity. What and who is born can often neither know nor be known by their parents, their descendants, sometimes not by their best friends, and definitely not by their enemies—those who, for whatever reason, seek to, and all too often succeed at, destroying. Destruction must be answered. There are crimes, and more and more these crimes seem to monstrously surpass all the laws and protections we have built up. The polis is a remembering. Beginnings are what we need to describe such facts, to start something new, to assure the world and each other that silence will never be forced upon us and that we will not give up on the world that is ours.

—Fred Dewey
Berlin, August, 2012

AMMIEL ALCALAY grew up in Boston and spent time in
Gloucester where family friends included Charles Olson
and Vincent Ferrini. High school, from 1969 to 1973, par-
ticularly when not in attendance, proved instructive. Through
the Grolier and Temple Bar Bookshops in Cambridge, he
befriended many poets, including John Wieners. Writing
came early and remained present despite many different
kinds of work, studies at City College, years abroad (living
in Jerusalem and sojourning in former Yugoslavia), and
completion of a doctorate in Comparative Literature, under
the tutelage of the late Allen Mandelbaum. Poet, novelist,
translator, critic, and scholar, Alcalay is Deputy Chair of the
PhD Program in English at the CUNY Graduate Center,
and former chair of Classical, Middle Eastern & Asian
Languages & Cultures at Queens College. Areas of academ-
ic involvement include American Studies, Comparative
Literature, Medieval Studies, and Middle Eastern Studies.
He was the first holder of the Lannan Visiting Chair in
Poetics at Georgetown University and has been a visiting
professor at Stanford University. His books include *a little
history* (re: public / UpSet, 2012), *"neither wit nor gold"(from
then)* (Ugly Duckling, 2011), *Islanders* (City Lights, 2010),
Scrapmetal: work in progress (Factory School, 2007),
Memories of Our Future: Selected Essays, 1982-1999 (City
Lights, 1999), and *After Jews and Arabs: Remaking Levantine
Culture* (University of Minnesota Press, 1993). During the
war in former Yugoslavia, he was one of the only transla-
tors working from Bosnian, and translated numerous
books and articles emerging directly from the war, includ-
ing books by journalist Zlatko Dizdarević and camp sur-
vivor Rezak Hukanović. Other translations include *Sarajevo
Blues* (City Lights, 1998) and *Nine Alexandrias* (City Lights,
2003) by Bosnian poet Semezdin Mehmedinović, *Keys to*

the Garden: New Israeli Writing (City Lights, 1996), and the co-translation (with Oz Shelach) of *Outcast* by Shimon Ballas (City Lights, 2007). With Megan Paslawski, he co-edited Michael Rumaker's *Robert Duncan in San Francisco* (City Lights, 2012). Along with Anne Waldman, he was one of the initiators of the Poetry Is News Coalition, and organized, with Mike Kelleher and Fred Dewey, the *OlsonNow* project. He is the founder and general editor, under the auspices of the PhD program in English and the Center for the Humanities at the CUNY Graduate Center, of *Lost & Found: The CUNY Poetics Document Initiative* (http://centerforthehumanities.org/lost-and-found).

BENJAMIN HOLLANDER emigrated from Haifa to Queens in 1958 at age six. He lives in San Francisco. He has published poetry, prose, and essays, and his books include: *Vigilance* (Beyond Baroque, 2005), *Rituals of Truce and the Other Israeli* (Parrhesia Press, 2004), *Levinas and the Police, Part 1* (Chax, 2001), *The Book of Who Are Was* (Sun & Moon, 1997), *How to Read, too* (Leech, 1992). As co-editor of the magazine *ACTS,* he also edited the special issue *Translating Tradition: Paul Celan in France* (1988). A novel, *In the House of Un-American*, is forthcoming in 2013 from Clockroot.

DIANE DI PRIMA is author of more than 40 books, including *This Kind of Bird Flies Backwards* (Totem Press, 1958), *Dinners and Nightmares* (Corinth, 1960; Last Gasp, 1998), *Memoirs of a Beatnik* (Olympia, 1968; Penguin, 1998), *Loba* (1978, 1998), *Pieces of A Song: Selected Poems* (City Lights, 1990), *Recollections of My Life As A Woman* (Penguin, 2001), and *Revolutionary Letters* (City Lights, 1971, 1974, 1979; Last Gasp, 2007). Founder and co-editor of the essential harbinger of the mimeo revolution *The Floating Bear*, founder of Poets Press and the Poets Theater, she was named Poet Laureate of San Francisco in 2009. Recent publications include *The Mysteries of Vision: Some Notes on H.D., R.D.'s H.D.*, and *Charles Olson Memorial Lecture*, all from *Lost & Found: The CUNY Poetics Document Initiative*. She is the subject of Melanie La Rosa's 2011 documentary *The Poetry Deal: A Film With Diane di Prima*, released by Women Make Movies.

FRED DEWEY's writings have been published internationally and his publications include *A Polis for New Conditions* (*Zen Monster,* 2011) and contribution to the anthologies *The Lowndes County Idea*, *The Architecture of Fear*, and *Most Art Sucks*. He directed Beyond Baroque Literary / Arts Center in Los Angeles from 1995-2010, building the Center's archive, and editing and publishing nineteen books there including the first publication of Simone Forti's *Oh, Tongue*, Ammiel Alcalay's *from the warring factions,* and anthologies including works by Jean-Luc Godard, Diane di Prima, Abdellatif Laabi, Daniel Berrigan, and others. He founded re: public in 2011.

UPSET PRESS

Theater of War: The Plot Against the American Mind
Nicholas Powers, 2005

The Comeback's Exoskeleton Matthew Rotando, 2008

Born Palestinian, Born Black & The Gaza Suite
Suheir Hammad, 2010

Halal Pork & Other Stories Cihan Kaan, 2011

Vocalises Jenny Husk, 2012

The Blond Texts & The Age of Embers Nadia Tueni
(translated by Amir Parsa), 2012

RE: PUBLIC

Oh, Tongue, by Simone Forti. New edition with post-script
by Jackson Mac Low. Edited with an afterword by Fred
Dewey. Forthcoming, 2013

RE: PUBLIC / UPSET

from the warring factions, by Ammiel Alcalay. New edition
with an introduction by Diane di Prima and conversation
with Benjamin Hollander. Edited by Fred Dewey, 2012

a little history, by Ammiel Alcalay. Edited with a foreword
by Fred Dewey, 2012

All UpSet Press titles can be ordered from upsetpress.org
or from its distributor the University of Arkansas Press.